PATHS TO POSITIVE AGING

DOG DAYS WITH A BONE
and Other Essays

Mary Gergen and Kenneth J. Gergen

Taos Institute Publications
Chagrin Falls, Ohio

Paths to Positive Aging

Dog Days with a Bone and Other Essays

Cover and Design Layout: Debbi Stocco

Library of Congress Catalog Card Number: 2016958962

Taos Institute Publications
A Division of the Taos Institute
Chagrin Falls, Ohio
USA

ISBN-10: 1-938552-50-4
ISBN-13: 978-1-938552-50-2

Printed in the USA and in the UK

Introduction to
Taos Institute Publications

The Taos Institute is a nonprofit organization dedicated to the development of social constructionist theory and practice for purposes of world benefit. Constructionist theory and practice locate the source of meaning, value, and action in communicative relations among people. Our major investment is in fostering relational processes that can enhance the welfare of people and the world in which they live. Taos Institute Publications offers contributions to cutting-edge theory and practice in social construction. Our books are designed for scholars, practitioners, students, and the openly curious public. The **Focus Book Series** provides brief introductions and overviews that illuminate theories, concepts, and useful practices. The **Tempo Book Series** is especially dedicated to the general public and to practitioners. The **Books for Professionals Series** provides in-depth works that focus on recent developments in theory and practice. **WorldShare Books** is an online offering of books in PDF format for free download from our website. Our books are particularly relevant to social scientists and to practitioners concerned with individual, family, organizational, community, and societal change.

— Kenneth J. Gergen
President, Board of Directors
The Taos Institute

For information about the Taos Institute and social constructionism visit:
www.taosinstitute.net

Table of Contents

A Welcome..7

I. FROM AGEISM TO POSITIVE AGING

Shedding our Ageism 10
Research and the Positive Reconstruction of Aging 13
The Sweet Symbolism of Being Senior 16
A Unique Joy of Aging 18
Reunions: Weaving, Marking, and Motivating 20
Recounting as Re-valuing 22
Memories as Resources 24

II. THINKING SMART

Enriching the Present Through the Past 28
Alzheimer's: A More Promising Look 31
Miraculous Awakening 34
Aging and the Enriching of Consciousness 36
The Mature Mind 38
Beware of "Acting Your Age" 41
What Does Research Really Tell Us About Decline 43

III. THE POSITIVE WAY

Whoever Laughs, Lasts 48
Aging as Art 50
Creating Positive Memories 52
The Power of Positive Questions 55
Dog Days, With a Bone 58
Resilience in Aging 61
Saying "No" to Aging 63
Respect and Renewal 65
Traveling Beyond Oneself 67
The Upside of Failure 69
From Turmoil to Tranquility 71
The Enchantment of Everyday Life 73

IV. SKILLS IN ACTION

Buddhist Practices For All Seasons 76

Exploring Time, Enriching Life 78

In My 75th Year 80

A Wild and Precious Life 82

Needed: Category Busters 84

The Call to Creativity 87

The Unsung Heroes 90

Respite and Renewal 92

Doing New Things Together 94

Life Beyond Achievement 97

The Third Age as the Creative Age 100

Reconstruction as Resource 102

V. RELATIONSHIPS: THE VITAL SOURCE

Gifts and the Valuing Process 108

Relational Life Review 110

Meditations on Relational Fire 112

Lighting the Fire of Relationships 114

Altruism: Lessons for the New Aging 116

The Rise of Senior Capital 118

Meaning in Life 121

Small Talk as Daily Bread 123

Aging and Physical Attraction: A Dialogue 125

The Power of Conversation 128

Benefits of Aging: Giving and Receiving 131

VI. LONGEVITY AND MORTALITY

Skills in Reconstructing and Relinquishing 134

Zest and Zing: If You Ain't Got That Swing 137

If Only I Were Younger 140

Positive Aging: Not all Smiley Faces 142

Reconstructing the Experience of Loss 145

About the Authors.. 147

A Welcome

This book is meant to provide good tidings for people who are pondering the aging process, and what it means for themselves and those they care about. It is composed of bite-sized essays in which we share ideas, inspirations, information, and personal experiences. All of these are devoted to developing and fortifying a positive perspective on growing old. Our aim is to bring to light resources—from science, professional practices, the news media, and our own experiences—that contribute to an appreciation of the aging process. Challenging the longstanding view of aging as decline, our hope is to kindle an appreciation of aging as an unprecedented period of human enrichment.

Each entry in this book is taken from essays we wrote for various editions of the *Positive Aging Newsletter* (www.positiveaging.net). In each of them we tried to capture an aspect of what it means for us to age in a positive way. The newsletter is guided by the view that aging is a social construction. That is, there is nothing about life itself that demands the idea of "aging" or "growing older." Nor is there anything about our bodily changes that commands us to see older bodies as somehow less attractive, less capable, or in general decline. Attractiveness, capability, and decline are not descriptions or pictures of who and what we are. They are interpretations, from a point of view. Other interpretations are possible. If this is so, why not orient toward those constructions that "get us the most," that give joy to life as opposed to anxiety and anguish? In effect, we want to celebrate aging, in all its manifestations.

Most of the essays in this book were written together. In the few cases, we have added the initial of the author. As you will also find, in a few essays we have invited others to participate. With each of the essays we have added a photograph. Almost all of them were taken by one of us, or someone in our family or friendship group. We hope they can add a visual dimension to the ideas we wish to share. The two of us have found the self-imposed demand of writing these essays to be deeply rewarding. It has required us to think more positively and creatively about the passing of days. We can only hope that some of these rewards can now be shared with you, the reader.

I. FROM AGEISM TO POSITIVE AGING

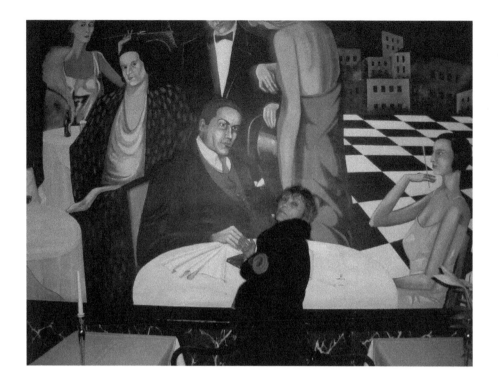

Shedding our Ageism

We have often written about the prevalence of ageism within the culture, and the problems it poses for the senior population. However, one of the frequently overlooked facts is that despite the repugnance of the negative stereotypes, most of us grew up embracing them. We laughed at the elderly ways, made jokes, and never ever wished to grow old. We and ageism were one. And most problematic: in spite of the repugnance of these stereotypes, we are not likely to have escaped their clutches. This is no small matter, because such beliefs can be deeply injurious to health and well-being.

Among the most subtle forms of ageism are commonly held views of what is proper behavior for older people. There are common sentiments against seniors being sexy, risk taking, flamboyant, or actively romping about; rather, they should be more reserved and quiescent. Relevant here is Kay Norman's view that one of the great unsolved puzzles from gerontology is why the vast majority of adults over 60 are basically couch potatoes. This is in spite of the general understanding that exercise is a major contributor to good health and longevity. As Norman reasons, the problem is primarily one of cultural beliefs.

Historically, people have always had to work very hard physically for their living. Farmers, laborers, and housewives had to put their shoulders to the grindstone every day of the year or suffer severe consequences. Whatever time could be spent in sedentary relaxation was considered the reward for a hard day's work. Nothing could beat the porch swing for physical pleasure. The advent of many labor saving devices also forged a strong link between financial success and reduced physical exertion. There was a clear distinction between laborers and "gentlemen" who did little physical work and between housewives and "ladies of the house" who had domestic help. There were also gender specific beliefs. In terms of play and sports, girls and women generally were discouraged from engaging in recreational exercise. Exercise was considered unladylike at best and harmful at worst; many young women were counseled by their doctors to avoid hard physical exertion for fear of damaging "female organs". Many men also have negative associations related to physical activity. Although boys were encouraged to be more physically active than girls, after a certain age physical activity just for fun was considered a frivolous use of time. *"A man with so much time and energy should be doing something productive"*, was the prevailing attitude.

This cluster of beliefs represents an indirect though powerful form of highly injurious ageism. Shedding such beliefs requires not only one's personal reflection and the concerted support of health professionals, but the strong engagement of our partners, our families, and our friends in creating new patterns of living. The health clubs, dance floors, athletic fields, and swimming pools should not be the private reserves of the young. Physical play will not only contribute to the well-being of all of us older people, but to future generations for whom earlier beliefs will become irrelevant.

Reference: Ageism—A barrier to healthy lifestyles by Kay Van Norman, *Journal on Active Aging*, Sept./Oct., 2004, 32-38.

Research and the Positive Reconstruction of Aging

Much traditional research on aging is based on the negative stereo-types of age in the culture at large. As widely assumed, "aging is a period of decline." If this is so, isn't it the task for researchers to chart this decline, to understand its severity, accelerating factors, and so on?

Isn't this what compassionate researchers should do? Although having its place, such research is not only narrow in its scope and conception, but simply fortifies the stereotype, and the common dread of growing old. If you study decline, it means you are both accepting the stereotype, and your findings will be all about decline. Researchers could do otherwise, and with a far more beneficial impact on society. As we see it, there are three major ways in which research can remove the straightjacket: A first step lies in RESISTANT ANALYSES of data, that is, analyses that do not terminate when the negative stereotype is confirmed. A good example is provided by Alwin and Ryan's research (2001) challenging the typical expectation that verbal ability declines with age. They showed that only a tiny portion of the decline could be accounted for by age alone. In contrast, differences in educational level proved to be the major predictor of decline. As one might expect, people with less education were less verbally proficient.

A major way of reversing the negative stereotype is through POSITIVE FOCUS. Instead of researching the extent to which a group of people might be declining or deteriorating, researchers could stress the positive aspects of their lives. To illustrate, early research indicated that aging people were more likely than younger ones to speak "off the topic" of conversation, a phenomenon researchers called "off topic verbosity." By changing the perspective to emphasize a positive focus, James and her colleagues (1998) demonstrated that this conversational pattern occurred primarily when people were describing events in their own lives. More positively, these reports were used by the elderly to emphasize the significance of their life-long experiences. These so-called diversions were serving a useful social function. Further, independent evaluators rated the stories told by older people more favorably than the leaner and duller stories of the young.

Third, researchers can CREATIVELY CONSTRUCT positive ways of understanding aging processes. As it is, researchers typically pick up a negative view that is already sensible, and then demonstrate its prevalence. Research on "cognitive loss" is a good example. But why not think outside the box, and develop new lenses of understanding. The extensive research on wisdom is a good example. Drawing from cultural history, the concept of wisdom opens a more uplifting way of viewing age changes in mental ability. In effect, research does not simply report on the world as it is; more importantly, it creates our understanding of the world.

References: D.F. Alwyn and J. M. Ryan, J. M. (2001). Aging, cohorts, and verbal ability. *Journal of Gerontology: Social Sciences. 56B,* S151-S161.
James, L.E., Burke, D. Austin, A and Hulme, E. (1998). Production and perceptions of "verbosity" in younger and older adults. *Psychology and Aging, 13,* 355-367.

The Sweet Symbolism of Being Senior

We once had the good fortune of attending a conference celebrating the 20th anniversary of the Kensington Consultation Centre. KCC was dedicated to providing assistance to individuals and organizations, and training future therapists and consultants. The audience for the event was largely composed of young students training in systemic theory. The speakers, in contrast, were largely individuals quite senior in years, men and women whose work had inspired the founding of the institution and set the intellectual tone for its development. What we found remarkable in these meetings was the deep dedication of the audience to these senior contributors. For the audience, their stories of the early years proved utterly fascinating; their accounts of their careers mesmerizing; and their current wisdom intriguing. In another session the audience told personal stories about experiences with seniors who had been inspirational to them.

For us these meetings demonstrated one of the most important and seldom recognized assets of aging: the sweet symbolism of being senior. We owe so much to those who are senior to us: parents, teachers, coaches, supervisors, bosses, religious leaders, and so on. And, while we often struggle for independence and may acquire our own legion of juniors, those above us occupy a special place of honor. It is just such individuals who have served as our life supports, our models, and our guides. It is they who have taken an interest in our well-being, applauded our successes, and nurtured us when we failed. With their stories we learn about where we came from, and invite us to reflect on what we will leave behind for others. Senior citizens are icons of deep and enduring significance. So today, if you feel you have gained senior status, celebrate your specialness.

A Unique Joy of Aging

We often like to think about aging as a stage of life, and like others, one that harbors both difficult challenges and openings to new and wonderful possibilities. As we moved from infancy to childhood, childhood to teens, and teens to adulthood, there were always struggles—pleasures disrupted and difficult learning curves to confront. Simultaneously there were great rewards—new possibilities, new pleasures, and so on. In this vein, as we write about positive aging, we like to emphasize the rewarding aspects of aging. So often these are swept aside as we recite the list of losses. We became especially aware of one unique pleasure of aging as we watched on television the final tennis match at Wimbledon. The championship match pitted the longstanding veteran Roger Federer against a much younger Novak Djokovic. The latter was at the top of the world's standings, and much favored. Indeed, after a grueling struggle, he won the match. From our viewpoint, however, what was so special about the entire tournament was how reverently the tennis gurus, the newspaper reporters, and the television commentators spoke of Federer. They showered him with compliments regarding his form, his versatility, his "cool," and his elegant play. Much this same respect was reflected in the crowd's support of Federer across the entire tournament.

In our view, this kind of respectful reverence is reserved for those who have made a sustained contribution to the world—great or small. Such a contribution may be highly visible, including the efforts of athletes, dancers, singers, musicians, and other artists who thrive, despite the competition from those who are younger. In military and economic ventures, in politics, religion, and law, the old warriors are revered for their long-term accomplishments.

However, the same may be said for many of the folks around us—those who have shown enduring character, love, dedication, sacrifice, generosity, and so on. These dear people acquire a special reverence, one that is unavailable to the young. Not only do they earn our deepest gratitude and respect, but they also symbolize hope for the future.

Reunions: Weaving, Marking, and Motivating

We just completed a season of class reunions during which there was a whole lot of talk about aging. Many people avoid reunions altogether, often for these very reasons. And we suffer a little when we meet dear friends from youth, bodies so altered by the years that they are unrecognizable. Then we shudder to think, "they don't recognize me either!"

And yet, we also found at these reunions a treasure trove of positive aging.

First, there was substantial evidence of life weaving, that is, of the way we have woven others and ourselves into a time-spanning tapestry. We find the early bonds were not just isolated episodes, cut away from the remainder of life. Rather, we carry these relations with us; they shaped us, taught us, and inspired our visions of the future. The friends of yore remain, silent and supportive companions of the road. For this we can be grateful.

The reunions also helped in age marking. That is, rather than our trying to deny that we are no longer youthful and that life is finite, there was a graceful marking of our maturity. There was a pervasive sense that "Life has been fulfilling, and I am fortunate to have lived it." There was also a challenge of the future. So many of our early friends were enthusiastic about adventures in the making, in travel, making art, volunteering, starting a new business, and more. Facing a limited future was not, then, an invitation to submission but to engage even more passionately in life's possibilities

In response to a 50th high school class reunion, one of us (MG) tried to capture some of these themes in the form of haikus. Here are several of them.

> Joy to reunite!
> Perhaps if we are lucky we find
> A lost self.

> Hard to believe, but here
> I make a new friend
> From an old acquaintance.

> Lined faces and old eyes
> Glide into youth
> As dusk darkens into night.

Recounting as Re-valuing

For many of us, the month of August is a nurturing interlude between seasons of teeming demands. Perhaps we have had time to visit with family and friends, and to re-connect with neighbors and acquaintances from years past. Most important, we have found the leisure to recount together events of the past—stories, humorous and sad, thrilling and disappointing. Often our story telling seems a way of simply spending pleasant time together. Sometimes we even repeat the same stories we have told each other for years. But the significance of this simple pastime is profound. A few weeks ago the two of us were on vacation with Wolfgang and Maggie, friends for over 35 years, but from whom we are separated by an ocean. We rented a house together in the countryside, and with long evenings to fill, storytelling became our entertainment. It is here we began to realize that as we laughed and moaned and were moved to silence by our library of well-worn stories, something important was taking place. Sure, there is mutual entertainment—laughter, joy, sadness, desire, and all the fruits of dramatic performance. But these stories also knit our lives together. We tell the stories of " When we bought the same sweatshirts at Sonia Rykiel in Paris", "We hid smelly cheese in each other's luggage", "Our kids babysat Little K", "We sang to Abba", and all of them silently affirm the bond of "we together." The stories also affirmed a world of shared values. Our favorite story of examining gravestones in the pouring rain is not simply a good yarn; it also gave rise to a research project that has made a difference in our lives, and produced what we felt were valuable outcomes for many others. So, there are real shortcomings in the common practice of focusing conversation on the here and now or to the next big thing. Looking backward together makes a significant contribution to our lives.

Memories as Resources

Perhaps I am naïve. I have spent the vast share of my life thinking forward. Somehow looking backward seemed a waste of time. I focus mainly on the activity right in front of me, and on what comes after that, and after that, and on into the future. It's always been, "what's coming" and "what to do about it?" Unless it was needed for one of my projects, looking backward seemed a useless daydream. Recently, however, I found myself in a situation where "looking forward" was useless. Mary and I were in Paraguay, and wanted to see the famous Iguazu Falls, a five-hour drive from where we were working. The van pulled up; Mary was placed in the front seat, and I in the back. I had hoped to read or work on my computer; so much to do. But the road was so bumpy, I found, that neither was possible. And the sounds of the road were so loud that conversation was also impossible. Soon the scenery became monotonous. For me, this was a condition bordering on hell!

I tried to doze, but the rumbling van would not allow for sleep. However, as I lay back with my eyes closed, I found myself slowly turning over incidents from the past in my mind. And when I began to recall an incident, I soon found myself reminiscing about an associated person, event or place. To my surprise, I slowly began to feel a sense of pleasure. I would say to myself, "That was a fun time"; "That was fascinating"; "He was terrific"; "She was fantastic".

With this, I began to focus on specific times and places—a sixth grade romance, senior prom, Paris in the 80's, and so on. I greeted old friends, smiled at mishaps, revisited feelings of awe…the time began to move swiftly; I had discovered a treasure.

Perhaps you as readers have known this pleasure all along. But for me it was another important step in realizing the joys of being older. We carry with us enormous riches, and if we learn to sort wisely through our memories, they are available at any moment to give us pleasure, support, companionship, affirmation, and more. Now I am going to invite Mary to go back and revisit those photo albums we have stored in our cupboard in the hall. They will help fill out the years that have been left as fallow fields. I worry that memories have been lost because I never visited them. I shall not wait for another bumpy ride to re-visit my treasure house. KJG

II. THINKING SMART

Enriching the Present Through the Past

|t is well recognized that memory is selective. We recall certain events as if they were yesterday; others slip into the dark. This is no small matter as we grow older. What if the memories that could enrich our daily lives, give us vitality, and cheer us on are among those that drop away? In our view, we do have some choice about this. We can actively contribute to the process of selecting memories. And we can do so in ways that sustain those that are life-giving. This fact was made so very clear to us this past December. Among the Christmas cards was a special letter. It was not the kind of report card letter that lets you know that everyone in the family earned an A+. Rather, Jane and Jon took a careful and caring look at specific events in the year. Each described, for example, an event that

was most exciting, another that was most gratifying, another that was most disappointing. And they each shared their favorite film, most enjoyable musical experience, moment of greatest beauty, and much more. We both enjoyed and were fascinated by their revelations. However, as we talked about the letter, we fell into unsettling reflection. How would we answer the questions that Jane and Jon had posed for themselves about what happened this past year? Yes, here and there a candidate memory came to mind—a special event, a vacation, and so on. However, all too often, and all too disappointingly, there was a blur. What were all the dinners with friends and families, the movies, and the special moments of pleasure or beauty? Tough questions, and a fear that much was lost forever.

The fact that Jane and Jon did manage to keep so much of the past in their working present led us to ponder: how could we help ourselves to make the past our daily companion? Most obviously, photographs can serve this function, but as photographic prints have become increasingly rare, so it seems has "showing and telling." And indeed, as the scholarly literature on "communal memory" suggests, one of the most important means of keeping the past vivid and vitalizing is through conversation. Those rollicking occasions when we trade tales of the past with family or friends are more than just fun. They knit past and present together, and weave the mix into our ongoing activities.

The two of us do experiment with ways of keeping the past alive. For example, when we travel we especially fear that the high points will be buried in the avalanche of demands confronting us on return. So, we spend time on the return trip reviewing what happened during the trip that was special, rewarding, or appreciated. Not only do we hope this will make these memories durable, but that the less than wonderful stuff will move into the dark. Now, stimulated by Jane and Jon, the two of us have also generated a joint computer file in which we can make entries whenever we are struck by an experience especially worth keeping. When we are on vacation we sometimes make little memory games for ourselves, like what are the five most beautiful beaches we have ever seen, the five most fun times with a grandchild, times when we have laughed the hardest…and so on. It's quite amazing how much good stuff we have stored away, if we would only go in search.

Alzheimer's: A More Promising Look

We commonly believe there is a disease called Alzheimer's and treat those who are ill as patients. In effect, we think of Alzheimer's as a medical illness, similar in nature to cancer or polio. Yet, there is growing opinion that such beliefs are both unwarranted and unhelpful. Consider, for example, the work of Peter Whitehouse, a doctor who has spent 30 years of professional life carrying out research, (including drug studies), reviewing medical journals, and treating those diagnosed with the disease. His conclusion is that the disease model is not only wrong, but inhumane and even immoral. In their recent book, *The Myth of Alzheimer's*, he and Daniel George suggest that we reconsider the aging process, particularly the normal ways in which the brain changes under various living conditions. Depending on such factor as physical and mental exercise, smoking, and diet, for example, these changes may be more or less debilitating. The dominant medical view is that this disease can be treated with drugs and that, with enough money, the pharmaceutical industry will provide the cure.

Rather, Whitehouse and George propose we would do better to focus on what we can do to improve our brain's health, accept that our bodies have limitations, and resist our biggest enemy as we age, fear! As they write, "Reframing Alzheimer's disease as brain aging and thus fundamentally altering the story we tell about cognitive loss can have profound effects on ourselves, our loved ones, our communities, our government policy, and our commerce. By placing ourselves on the continuum of brain aging and seeing it as a lifelong undertaking rather than an end-of-life 'disease' we'll find solidarity with all the vulnerable members in our society—from our children to our elders." Other professionals support and extend this view. Anthea Inne's *Dementia Studies*, also stresses the importance of challenging assumptions. She looks especially at the political, economic, social and cultural issues that influence the perspectives on patients and their caregivers. She sees a common degradation of people with dementia, one that affects how they are cared for, and how their caregivers feel about helping.

This concern with stereotyping is extended in Lisa Snyder's *Speaking our Minds: What it's like to have Alzheimer's*. The Alzheimer's diagnosis, in her view, invites an insensitivity to the patient's capacities for awareness and for their needs and desires. Those people interviewed by Snyder speak of their fear, challenges, social support systems, feelings of loneliness, means for overcoming their limits, and the joy they experience in their lives—despite their diagnosis. Perhaps the last feeling is the most surprising to those of us who take a "poor you" stance when it comes to thinking of those who are labeled as having dementia. Snyder says of her interviewees that they "reminded me of how quickly we measure disability, deficits and differences at the risk of overlooking ability, strengths and commonality" (pg. 34). Among the strengths she notes, is the ability to find in a situation something of value, even if you need someone to help you eat. Snyder suggests that in framing stories of loss, the public reinforces a malignant stereotype. Rather than this, we should understand that all people have capacities that can bring joy to relationships, if we can be sensitive and creative enough to bring these capacities to fruition.

Miraculous Awakening

We thank Brian McCaffrey for sending us one of the most unsettling and inspiring videos we have seen in some time. In the first few moments, we found the video difficult to watch. We are exposed to an aged and nearly toothless woman, Gladys Wilson, who is diagnosed with Alzheimer's. Beyond some primitive bodily movements, she seems completely unavailable to others. Enter Naomi Feils, a diminutive, older woman who practices what she calls validation therapy. She approaches Gladys with a kind voice and gentle touch. Slowly, through a combination of touching, singing, and coordinating movements, Gladys begins to respond. With Naomi's continued patience and a caring dedication, Gladys suddenly begins to sing along with Naomi. She grasps Naomi's hands and draws her close; soon their faces are touching. And, almost magically, Gladys begins speaking with Naomi. For us, it was like watching someone raised from the dead.

Surely this video inspires hope for those whose loved ones have been diagnosed with Alzheimer's. However, we also found in this video a poetic analogue. There is a way in which the work-a-day world of adult life can be brain deadening. That is, the continuing routines and requirements of adult life have a way of narrowing one's capacities to respond to the world.

One comes to feel that his or her personality has solidified, that he or she is a "certain kind of a person." The range of tastes, appreciations, and curiosities is reduced. Certain persons or activities cease to matter. As we see it, this is a dangerous attitude with which to enter the retirement years. With fewer work or family demands, one is left with the potentially deadening sense of a fixed and final way to be in the world. Yet, it is not so easy to simply pull yourself up by your own bootstraps; how can we imagine ourselves being other than what we are? So perhaps we should be on the look-out for the Naomi Feils of everyday life, those people who may remind us of our "singing selves," and inspire new and invigorating dialogues among us. One may also practice Naomi Feil's validation therapy with others who seem to languish in the world. Our mutuality of touch, and song, and voice may free us all from our forms of solitary confinement.

Reference: Gladys Wilson and Naomi Feil—YouTube http://www.youtube.com/watch?v=CrZXz1oFcVM

Aging and the Enriching of Consciousness

Rather than fretting over what seem to be the losses in aging, we try to focus on the rewards. We look for ways to challenge the pervasive and debilitating construction of age as decline, and to kindle a deeper appreciation of this time of life. We have recently been struck by what we feel is the way aging enriches our conscious experience. There are at least two forms of this enrichment, one a sharpening and the other a layering of our daily life experiences. In the case of the sharpening we think about appreciative attention. Here we draw on the words of the novelist Martin Amis, from a recent *New York Times* interview, "Life grows in value...Not very significant things suddenly look very poignant and charming. This particular period of my life is full of daily novelty. That turns out to be worth a great deal." Perhaps this kind of appreciation is hastened by the growing awareness of the finite. When life appears endless, one scarcely savors the passing moment; when the end is closer at hand, each moment bursts with flavor.

In the case of layering, the everyday world becomes animated by our histories. A coffee cup may not simply be a cup sitting there on the table, for example. It may vibrate with memories—of the friend who brought it as a gift; the design that reminds you of a vacation in France, and your mother who always admired these ceramics. Layer upon layer of memory, enriched by images and emotion. This same layering of experience is there in the hydrangea bush, the arrival of the Sunday paper, the dining room carpet, the rake and the shovel, and so on. Simply walking around each day can set before us a feast of experience cooked up by the chef of memory. Such enrichment also gains by virtue of contrast. When one has lived through life's many challenges—its glories and its agonies—the meaning of the moment is not exhausted in itself. Rather, one can experience it in terms of its similarities and contrasts with other times. A man is not simply holding a grandchild on his lap, for example. He may also be aware of a "new beginning," "the sustaining of a tradition," "a changing relationship to his own offspring—now a father or mother," and "the creation of a new identity" for himself. At these moments, we may smile deeply in ways that those with fewer years under their belts could not possibly understand.

The Mature Mind

The assumption that the biology of aging is inherently a biology of decline is widespread, and indeed is the central rationale for much research. It is thus enormously refreshing to discover a broad based account of aging that takes the opposite perspective. To be sure, abundant research does suggest a general though relatively minor decline in rapid information processing. However, as Gene Cohen proposes in his book, *The Mature Mind*, such research misses a very important process of positive development. Namely, the biology of aging favors the development of a talent we might well call wisdom.

Cohen lodges portions of his argument in neural research. For example, he cites the abundant research demonstrating that the brain remains quite flexible with age, and new neural connections are always being made. In addition, however, he finds research indicating that with advancing age people can increasingly rely on both sides of the brain to do various cognitive tasks. This sets them apart from the young. With this increased balance, argues Cohen, older people are more capable than the young in: 1. *Relativistic thinking* (accepting uncertainty, suspending judgments), 2. *Dualistic thinking* (holding a view and its opposite possibility), and 3. *Systematic thinking* (seeing the bigger picture, the forest as well as the trees). These are major characteristics of mature thought.

Adding depth and dimension to his research, Cohen has studied over 3,000 older adults by using interviews and questionnaires over the years. To elaborate his view of maturity more fully, he proposes four stages of mature development. The first is *Midlife Re-evaluation* during the 50s and 60s, which is a time for exploration and transition (Where have I been? Where do I wish to go?) Such a stage need not generate a crisis; in its most positive form it yields a sense of continued quest. Next is a *Liberation phase*, in the 60s and 70s, (I am not a victim of my past. The time for action is now. If not now, when?). After these explorations, there may be a *Summing up* phase. Here one may review one's life, resolve tensions, and integrate old and new activities and relationships. This may be a time to create memoirs, and for many, to give back to the family, community, or world. Finally one may experience a stage of *Encore*, which may involve a continuing desire to go on, even in the face of adversity or loss.

For Cohen, aging should be viewed with positive anticipation. It is a period that can usher in greater engagement, more satisfying intellectual growth, and more fun. Retirement is not over the hill, but a time for climbing new hills. Yet, positive transitions are not guaranteed by biology. If one doesn't use one's capacities they may be lost. Among his recommendations for positive aging are:

- Forming active links with the surrounding community

- Balancing group activities with solo ones, energetic action with relaxation

- Increasing levels of activity over time; add to one's activities rather than subtract

- Locating long duration activities, and not simply short term or one-time adventures

- Nourishing close friendships

- Approaching learning as a life-long activity

In sum, Cohen offers an informative and inspiring account of maturity. We applaud the effort.

Reference: *The Mature Mind* by Gene D. Cohen, M.D., Ph.D. NY: Perseus, 2005.

Beware of "Acting Your Age"

H ere we share one of the most important research findings we have yet discovered: Researchers at Yale University's Department of Epidemiology and Public Health carried out a longitudinal study of 660 people over the age of 50. First they were asked about their agreement with the popular stereotypes that as you grow older you lose your pep, things get worse, you are less useful, and you are less happy. Researchers then tracked the sample for decades. One of the significant questions was related to longevity. Would accepting or refuting stereotypes of aging make a difference in terms of who lived and who died? Quite remarkably, they found that those who disagreed with the stereotypes lived seven-and-one half years longer than those who agreed with them. This is a greater gain in longevity than that associated with low blood pressure, low cholesterol, a healthy weight, abstaining from smoking, or exercising regularly!

We were recently reminded of these findings and their importance when a reader introduced us to the Red Hat Society (www.redhatsociety. com). The society, an informal group of some 25,000 chapters began, as Sue Ellen Cooper, the "Queen Mother" of the group describes, "a result of a few women deciding to greet middle age with verve, humor and elan." The red hat and purple clothing that is worn in fun by the group, is inspired by Jenny Joseph's poem, "Warning," which contains the lines:

When I am an old woman I shall wear purple

With a red hat which doesn't go and doesn't suit me.

There are important implications here for the aging population and all those professionals who work with them. Specifically, there are important benefits to be derived from "breaking the rules," from acting in ways that challenge the common stereotypes of age as a diminished stage of life. Nothing should be given up because it "isn't fitting for people our age." Challenging the stereotypes may not only add zest to life, but add years to the lifespan. Have you always wanted to learn the tango, take up scuba diving, see the dawn from the night-side, visit an Ashram, camp in the wilderness, write poetry, or go deep-sea fishing? Maybe it's time to "practice a little now." A longer life may be our reward. And besides, if increasing numbers join in breaking the common expectations, so may we kindle the anticipation of the younger generations for what is ahead. The "cloud of aging" may be lifted.

Reference: Longevity increased by positive self--perceptions of aging by Becca R. Levy, Martin D. Slade, Suzanne R. and Stanislov V. Kasl. *Journal of Personality and Social Psychology*, 2002, *83*, 261--270

What Does Research Really Tell Us About Decline

f you scan the contents of most gerontology research journals, you will find numerous articles on age deficits. These articles reveal declines in virtually all areas of life. Of course, these reports also feed the negative stereotypes of aging so pervasive in the culture, along with the fear of aging so common to so many. Even worse, research has shown that people who think positively about getting older live longer than those who think negatively. How, then, can we reduce the impact of deficit research on the negative stereotypes and associated fears? At least one important way is to realize the substantial limitations of research on aging. When we come to realize the weaknesses, some of the weights caused by the fear of aging can be lifted. We focus here on six of these. While we emphasize research on cognitive deterioration, the problems are inherent in most research on age decline:

Trivial differences. Research may reveal statistically significant decline in various laboratory tasks, but these differences may well be trivial in terms of their significance in everyday life. For example, a statistically significant difference between younger and older research subjects of one second in reaction time might be demonstrated in the ability to read and comprehend a page of newsprint. You might ask, however, whether it would make any difference in one's life if it required 2 seconds more to read the front page of a newspaper at the age of 80 than it did at 40. Without a substantial case for the social significance of the kinds of decline demonstrated in the laboratory, such research is more smoke than fire.

Trivial capacities. Many measures of cognitive deficit are developed in the laboratory. Special apparatus are often constructed to measure these deficits. Elder subjects often respond less adequately than their younger counterparts on such apparatuses. However, it is often quite unclear how performance on these measures can be translated into actions in everyday life. For example, does reacting more slowly to a split second flash of light in a laboratory apparatus have any important implications for living effectively? How often do we confront a situation in which we must respond within milliseconds to a flashing light? Sometimes it is the weirdness of the laboratory situation itself that may throw off older adults, who have not been required to participate in psychology experiments as undergraduates.

Misjudging the Cause. Virtually all studies of decline are attributed to age differences. Yet, as gerontology researchers are quite aware, age itself does not cause anything. In effect, the age variable serves as a cover for the fact that we generally do not know the causes of such declines. This means that all studies of decline stand open to alternative explanations. And among these alternatives are much more optimistic ways of viewing lifespan changes. For example, there are hundreds of studies demonstrating memory declines with age. However, the older person has also accumulated far more information over a lifetime than the young. Memory decline may not result from age, but from the fact that one has a far greater corpus of information at his or her disposal. It is harder to get to the right piece of information as quickly as one who has less.

Over-generalization. In most studies of decline negative findings are interpreted as if they apply to the entire samples, let's say of people who are 20–40 compared to 60–80. However, such findings neglect what are typically wide individual variations in each group. The overlap between the younger and the older group may be very large. Many people in the older groups are more capable than many in the younger. This fact is typically hidden by analyzes of mean differences.

Biased Search. Researchers do not measure everything. They begin their research looking for specific outcomes. Because of the problem-centered focus of most research foundations, researchers are motivated to search for deficits. If deficits can be located, alarms may be sounded! The result is a litany of grief; all systems seem to be deteriorating. However, researchers have yet to make significant efforts to explore the positive potentials of aging. With increased effort to locate such potentials, they would certainly be discovered.

Contextual Insensitivity. Researchers often assume that declines are inevitable. If they demonstrate a loss in reaction time, they often presume that such losses are intrinsic to the process of aging—a natural trajectory. However, such assumptions are typically without merit. Our skills at any time in life are importantly wedded to the demands of the time. If the demand for rapid information processing ceases at retirement, chances are that the skill will taper off. If the demand continues, the skill is likely to remain strong. Infrequently do researchers target ways in which skills may be increased or enriched during the later years.

The stereotypical conclusion that aging means decline is an easy one; it is also the most dangerous in its effects on society. Decline in aging should not be embraced as the first conclusion, but rather the last.

III. THE POSITIVE WAY

Whoever Laughs, Lasts

We were recently struck by a line from the poet W.H. Auden, "Among those I like or admire, I can find no common denominator, but among those I love, I can: all of them make me laugh." For us this underscored the central importance of laughter in our lives, and in our relationships. Researchers have long touted the contribution of laughter to our physical and psychological well-being. As amply demonstrated, laughter improves respiration, lowers blood pressure, relaxes the muscles, improves brain functioning, and reduces pain. Many believe it also strengthens the immune system. And in laughing, tensions and anxieties are reduced, anger dissipates, and our disposition improves.

However, with Auden, we also see laughter as playing a central role in relationships themselves. We don't feel that laugher is essential to love, but we do find ourselves drawn to those with whom we laugh. To laugh together is, first of all, a sign of trust. To laugh with a person's antics is to support his or her parting with common convention. Laughing together is also a form of mutual play, one that allows us to reveal fuller personalities—as children, comedians, buffoons, pranksters, and the like. As a couple we have often found our way out of a brewing disagreement with a humorous remark.

Finally, we have written much over the years about the capacity to see events from many perspectives. While "growing old" is a drag; to see it as "growing wise" is a gift. Humor is a pivotal means of "seeing anew." Humor is an escape from the prison of realism. The difference between a stumbling block and a stepping-stone may be a ready quip.

Aging as Art

t's often been said that life copies art, but I recently found myself asking what if we looked at life itself as an art form? More to the point, what could we learn or appreciate if we could see aging as an art? I especially liked this idea, as it seemed a great alternative to the common metaphor of "aging as over the hill!" But a lot depends on what form of art you select, and where it is applied. So, I asked, what if I just looked at each day as a blank canvas and myself as the artist. How could I paint the day so that it could be interesting or beautiful? This was a pleasant thought over the morning's coffee, but I must confess that as the day started rolling, the image went on holiday. That seemed only fair, because it was also a holiday for me, and a beautiful day at that. So, I invited Mary to join me for an afternoon of golf. The afternoon began poorly.

Although guaranteed a clear start, we were placed behind two more parties at the first hole. And while waiting impatiently, another party arrived behind us. Ugh! This meant that our every swing would be observed by the folks behind us. This might be ok if you were a seasoned golfer, assured of making impressive shots. But we are rank amateurs, and being watched is nerve wracking. Thus, when it finally came time for my first shot, I promptly drove the ball into the side of a nearby house! Then the tedium set in, as the play was interminably slow, and the sun had now become quite hot. By the third hole, I was in very poor spirits, and poor company for Mary. Slowly we were becoming alienated. I slunk into silence, depressed at the thought of the afternoon now spread before us.

But then, in a flash, the blank canvas metaphor returned. "If this is your painting of the day, I said to myself, "you are one lousy artist!" With this, I turned to Mary and proposed that we create the rest of the afternoon in a different way. We laughed, the tension was broken, and we just relaxed and enjoyed the beautiful scene. (Interestingly, our play improved as well). In retrospect, my feeling is that the world may come to us in many forms, but we have control of the colors. And it is in the painting that we can create worlds worth waking up for. KJG

Creating Positive Memories

In many ways, aging positively is a skill. Just as successful childhood required that we learn the skills to excel in school, so do other periods of life demand that we expand our capacities. In later years, one skill of important to well-being is that of creating positive memories. On the face of it, this may sound odd. After all, we traditionally believe, memory is memory. It simply functions to record what has happened to us. If we have positive experiences we will have positive memories; if we have suffered on many occasions, our memories will reflect this fact.

Yet, recent decades of research on memory refute such a view. Rather, we find, memory is highly elastic. What we recall about past events can shift dramatically from one context to another. If the conditions are right, people can be induced to recall a crime they have committed, even though they never did so. And how often do siblings recall something that happened to them in childhood, only to find out that it happened to a brother or sister? In effect, memory is not simply a fading imprint of the past; we have some control over what we carry with us in the way of personal history.

As we move into the later years of life, issues of memory are particularly acute. Increasingly we come to understand ourselves in terms of our past lives, for example, what we have accomplished, contributed to, overcome, or experienced as joy or pleasure. Conversely, we confront our failures, missed opportunities, sorrows, and pain. Whether we are comforted and inspired, on the one hand, or suffer guilt, remorse, or a sense of emptiness on the other, depends on our capacity to cultivate our memories. It takes skill to keep the positive foremost, while avoiding the dead weight of negative experience. If we can "do it right," our memories of the past can buoy our spirits, kindle our enthusiasms, and furnish a supportive sense of purpose. If we simply let "the past be the past," we risk finding ourselves uninspired, alienated, and depressed. The two of us do not have a convenient check-list for cultivating positive memories. Much like painting in oils, people find many different ways of reaching desired ends. Ideally, there should be ways of drawing widely from each other's experiences. Perhaps the internet will ultimately provide a means of exchanging our grass-roots knacks for living well. In the meantime, we offer several suggestions from our own collective experiences:

Telling stories. Our understanding of our pasts is largely generated through the way we talk about it—both to others and ourselves. These narratives will highlight certain details and obliterate others; they will emphasize certain outcomes and suppress others; they will create the value that we place on the past. Thus, to tell good stories to others about what has happened to us is to generate a positive resource for living. We often do this together after we have been on trips. We review the journey specifically in terms of what we enjoyed or learned or felt good about; we simply don't talk about the frustrations and failures. At the same time, it is also possible to take a calamity or failure and turn it into amusement for family or friends. Sometimes when we confront troubles, we say to each other, "What a great story this will make." Calamity is reconstructed as a social resource.

Sorting images. Often our records of the past are sustained with images—photographs and films. Such images vary enormously in the feelings they elicit. On the one hand, we may shudder to see how we looked on a given occasion, or recall how badly the pictured event turned out. Other images generate a sense of happiness, love, pride, and so on. All image archives are necessarily selective. The challenge is to select out for the long-term those images that sustain a positive or meaningful register of living. (When our children were young, we discarded photographs in which one or more of them looked particularly unsightly or miserable. We didn't want to encourage any sad stories of how they grew up.)

Displaying artifacts. In the same way that narratives and images create a particular sense of the past, so do various artifacts—souvenirs, paintings, clothing, books and so on. A room with bare walls and nothing in the way of curious objects is a room that destroys history. The psychoanalyst Carl Jung once reasoned that the objects and images about us are extremely important in evoking the past and enriching the present. In effect, they can generate a sense of the past that is supportive and sustaining. Those are not knick-knacks on the shelf; they are resources for a spirited life.

The Power of Positive Questions

We often encounter a poster featuring a wizened senior who says, "Growing old is not for sissies." One implication is, of course, that aging is a tough experience to endure. It is all about decline. And thus we so often find ourselves asking whether we are OK. Is my memory still ok? Can I still think clearly? Have I lost my stamina? Am I still attractive? The list goes on and on.

These questions may seem natural enough, but they are not necessary, and they are not good friends. As our family therapist colleagues say, "The problem is the problem." By this they mean that when we start to inquire into our problems, we begin to construct a world in which problems are central. They become the dominant realities that burden every day. In effect, the questions we ask ourselves are self-creating. To ask about our failings is to create a world in which failing is a real possibility. Yet, this same logic also holds enormous potential. By asking ourselves positive questions we may bring forth future action of far greater promise.

Organizational change agents working with a process called Appreciative Inquiry know this very well. Drawing from their work in organizational development, Frank Barrett and Ron Fry phrase it this way:

"The questions we ask determine whether we eventually diminish our capacity to grow and develop, or increase it." The work in organizational change applies no less in everyday life.

This is the lesson to be drawn from the work of Jacqueline Stavros and Cheri Torres in their book, *Dynamic Relationships, Unleashing the Power of Appreciative Inquiry in Daily Living.*

For example, they propose that in our relationships with others we focus our discussions on such questions as: What is working?

What gives life to the relationship?

How does the way we relate increase our success?

Stimulated by these ideas we ourselves have tried to put them into action. For example, when the extended family meets for dinner, we begin the meal by having each person, young and old, say something about what they appreciate about the day. It is amazing how this sharing animates dialogue, and how much good will bursts forward. One of us (KJG) experienced an early trauma in public speaking. As a child he was unable to find his carefully written speech as he stepped up to address a crowd of parents and teachers. To this day the panic sometimes returns just before his public speaking engagements. The antidote: quietly ask oneself to recall all those occasions in which public speaking was a success.

Such positive questions have other good effects. For one, we are less inclined to find fault in others. When we feel ok about ourselves we don't have to bolster our confidence by looking for the ways we are better than others. Given the increasing evidence that optimism and longevity walk hand in hand, there is more good reason to ask positive questions. Rather than asking about what is failing or declining, we may can ask questions that focus on what we appreciate in life, who and what needs our help, what sources of joy can be found in the day ahead? Growing old well is for the wise, and when we are fully wise we understand that positive questions are always at our fingertips.

References: Barrett, F.J. and Fry, R.E. (2005) *Appreciative Inquiry, A positive approach to building cooperative capacity.* Chagrin Falls, OH: Taos Institute Publications.
Stavros, J.M. and Torres, C.B. (2005) *Dynamic relationships, Unleashing the power of appreciative inquiry in daily living.* Chagrin Falls, OH: Taos Institute Publications.

Dog Days, With a Bone

Mary and I spend a great deal of time searching materials highlighting the positive side of aging. We prize anything we can find that helps to construct the last third of life as a period of unprecedented enrichment. But what about the challenge of actually living life in this way? So often, it simply doesn't seem realistic. What's so positive, we ask ourselves, about illness, the loss of capacities, loneliness, and so on? Well, this past month I had an opportunity to directly confront the beast. It was mid-August, and time for vacationing at the shore with the family—swimming, tennis, golf, walks on the beach, excursions with the grandchildren, and all the rest. However, just days before the anticipated holiday, while playing tennis with friends, I leaped for a ball that was out of reach, and rip! My Achilles tendon was nearly shorn in two. There was first the searing pain, and then the long dull pain, followed by the pain produced by trying to walk in the large boot/cast that was to be my companion for the next six weeks. There was to be no vacation, as I would be confined to a chair, with long periods of lying prone with my leg hoisted in the air. Hot, humid, dull, dog days. So, these were the cruel facts; a "positive approach" indeed! Or, at least, so it felt for a time.

But there is in the mediation world a concept of "double listening." This means, one should pay attention not only to the dominant story a client is telling, but to subtle signals that there is a second, untold story lying behind. I soon began to find my own signs of an untold story behind the obvious tale of misery. There was first the fact that the confinement meant that I could make headway in the staggering stack of demands that usually colored my daily life with guilt. I could welcome a certain lightness of heart. And, lying there on the bed, foot propped in the air, I began digging into several books I had longed to read. Within days, I realized that I was entering a period of significant calm, a lovely feeling of balanced centeredness that a family vacation could never offer. In this space I also found a creative space was opening; new and inspiring ideas began to take shape. There were also the more guilty pleasures of being relieved from household duties, finding people waiting on me, and being ushered to the head of lines. And each day there were positive voices—nurturing and supportive. Hmm…should I plan now for an annual injury to replace the normal vacation? No, but I can see how, with more discerning eyes, our dog days can be supplemented with a delicious bone. KJG

Resilience in Aging

A most welcome addition to our library is a recent book edited by Prem Fry and Corey Keyes called *New Frontiers in Resilient Aging*. These well-known authorities in gerontology brought together major researchers to discuss the nature of resilience, and how this capacity influences our lives as we age. Resilience may be described in many ways, but we would define it as the ability to overcome challenging circumstances. Like the proverbial rubber ball, resilience is the capacity to bounce back. The authors in this book believe that most older people are able to capitalize on their long experience of living to continue to grow, learn, and enjoy life, in spite of the difficult challenges confronted along the way. As the chapters of the book demonstrate, great assets for remaining resilient include:

- Valuing your relationships

- Involving yourself in committed to projects and causes

- Staying open to new experiences

- Having people in your life who care about you

- Searching for intellectual stimulation.

In the final chapter in this volume, the two of us explored the idea that a major resource for resilience lies in our capacity to reconstruct or reframe events in our lives. For example, it is common to view what we call "decline in physical and mental abilities," "physical handicaps," or "reduced physical attractiveness" in a negative way. All are considered deficits, and if accepted, this definition of our daily lives carries an extra weight. We are doomed! However, in our workshops, we have challenged our participants to reconsider ways in which each of these deficits could also contribute to their lives. From the lively conversations that follow, participants are able to generate new and far more promising ways of seeing such events.

What some see as decline in abilities, can also be viewed as an invitation to new and more tranquil ways of life; reduced attractiveness also releases one from worrying about a whole set of complex issues of relating; and so on. If we can remain flexible in our constructions of self and world, so can we move more ably through the choppy waters of life.

Reference: Fry, P S. and Keyes, C. L. M. (Eds.) *New Frontiers in Resilient Aging: Life-Strengths and Well-Being in Late Life*. (2010). New York: Cambridge University Press.

Saying "No" to Aging

How we age is very much related to our social lives. As Harvard psychologist Ellen Langer proposes in her book, *Counterclockwise*, we are all potential victims of negative stereotypes about aging and health; too often we accept these stereotypes, and this shapes both our conceptions of self and our behavior. Consider, for example, her early research. Here she brought a group of men who were in their 70's and early 80's to an old New England hotel. In the hotel she created a time warp scene; as in a theatrical play, all the props told the men that it was 20 years earlier, which was when they were in their 50's and 60's. They were instructed not to reminisce, but to act as though they had traveled back in time. Langer's findings were stunning: After just one week, the men in the experimental group (compared with controls of the same age) had more joint flexibility, increased dexterity, and less arthritis in their hands. Their mental acuity had risen measurably, and they had improved gait and posture. Photographs taken of the men at the hotel were rated by outsiders as significantly younger. In another study, Langer investigated the impact of our clothing on our aging process. She looked at the differences between those people who wear uniforms at work, versus those who don't. Her reasoning was that uniforms mask the ages of the wearers and do not offer cues to others or to oneself about age. As she found, those in uniform missed fewer days of work owing to illness or injury, had fewer doctor visits and hospitalizations, and had fewer chronic diseases.

Despite these results, we may not want to dig out our old miniskirts and bell bottoms, but they do suggest that we consider both context and appearance in terms of how we live our lives. Rather than spending our time and dressing according to the stereotypes of what an "old person" should do, we should spend our time and dress according to what we most desire, despite the wicked urge to conform. As commonly said, you are as old (or young) as you act.

Respect and Renewal

For two weeks we have been traveling in India. A series of lectures offered moments of adventure, intense involvement, and also reflection. This was especially so, as we entered the surrounding culture, and particularly as we explored the Indian traditions of aging. Here we were struck with the strong value placed on "filial piety," that is, a deep respect for elders. We met a young professional, for example, who traveled two hours each way from home to his place of work. We asked why he and his wife did not move closer to his work. He responded that they lived with his parents, and he did not wish to be away from them. Should he ever move, he would ensure they came with him. A young bride told us, "It is comforting to live together with my in-laws. They are older and wiser than we are, and they give us advice and support when we are trying to decide about things." Supported by government policies, the family is the central unit of care and throughout one's life, it is a principle source of meaning. Children must care for their parents and adhere to their teachings. Yet, this tenet is under stress in India, especially as the young leave home to expand their horizons abroad. Upon returning home our thoughts began to focus on the sources of respect for the aging population in our culture. Filial piety is scarcely a major value in American's society today.

Further, the fast-paced changes in the technologies of daily living (e.g. television, internet, mobile phones) generate a growing knowledge gap between the young and the old. Yet there remain many resources through which respect for older people can be found. For one, we all carry with us repositories of respect stretching back to childhood—we recall the respect we received from our parents, teachers, friends, colleagues, and so on-all readied for our revisiting whenever required. And there is the surrounding cohort of family and friends, whose respect and regard may be staples of everyday life. We also carry repositories of wisdom and insight that stand as vital resources for the younger generations. And, by sustaining our creative and caring activities—within our families, our friendship and civic groups, through voluntary commitments and political activity, in our philanthropy, and so on—we kindle the fires of respect, and provide models for future generations.

Traveling Beyond Oneself

We recently returned from a two-week lecturing stint at Ritsumeikan University in Kyoto, Japan. This provided some splendid opportunities to visit the ancient temples and shrines that adorn this precious city, stroll the busy shopping streets, explore the forests and riversides, and meet with friends and colleagues to dine on traditional tatami mats. We counted ourselves so very fortunate. Yet, hovering about these experiences was also a certain sense of unease. We are scarcely alone in our enjoyment of world travel. And indeed, most people list travel somewhere toward the top of their list of post-retirement plans. In effect, the world is filled with thousands of us imbibing the pleasures of the world's museums, gardens, theaters, forests, monuments, restaurants, and so on. But consider: is it sufficient that the sum effect of these efforts is simply personal pleasure? Are these merely consummatory acts similar to eating an ice-cream cone or watching a comedy? The question is all the more plaguing, as such travels often leave a heavy footprint of carbon. Do we satisfy our curiosity at the world's expense?

A contemplative moment at the Myoshinji temple, a home of Zen Buddhism, prompted a more promising vision: As Buddhists reason, meditation is not an end in itself. Rather, afterwards, one experiences a renewed and compassionate sense of connection with others and the world. Could we not understand our privileged indulgence in the world's treasures in a parallel way? It is not just the impact of these experiences on the pleasure center of our brains that is important. Rather, it is the capacity of these experiences to continue their flow-through us and into surrounding the world-that grants them special significance. To experience beauty, serenity, wonder, deeper understanding, and a new appreciation of others is to leave us with new capacities to create and share with others. When these experiences add to our support of the arts; hospitality to foreign visitors; sharing with others what we have learned to appreciate; or investments in world peace, the experiences are magnified. When we share these with our children and their families, our gifts are multiplied as they carry them on. We share in creating the ripple effects of the world's cultural treasures, and their potential to create a more enriched future for all.

The Upside of Failure

We so often hear the expression, "I'm too old to do that." Each time people say this, they close the door on an opportunity that could be expanding, enriching, and enlivening.

People restrict themselves when it comes to travel, athletics, education, volunteer activities, cultural events, and more. It even happens when it is about relationships. A friend at a class reunion exclaimed that she was too old to consider a romantic relationship—"not at my age," she said. For many, aging also seems to bring about a sense of fear and failure. I recently read about a series of interviews in which highly successful entrepreneurs were asked to account for their success. Among the most prominent answers was the willingness to take risks. This also led to the obvious corollary that failing was also crucial to their success. As reasoned, one *learns from failure*, gains new insights, and acquires valuable experience. I started thinking about my family's opinions of my birthday cake baking skills. My birthday cakes have long been the butt of jokes among our kids. There was the plastic-like chocolate frosting that cracked off in pieces, and the angel food cake that had to be scraped out of the pan, the one the ants found first, and so on. But, interestingly no one failure was repeated! Over the years I have learned a lot about cake baking. Today, I can make a passable birthday cake. Failure provided the means for growth and learning, and along the way, I gave the family a lot of laughs. Had I given up and searched for the nearest bakery, life would have been less rewarding.

Perhaps it is a good time to consider some new risks. Bronco busting may not be at the top of my list, but the challenges of new technologies, educational opportunities, arts and dance, exotic travel, and political involvement are almost always at hand. Ken is asking me to join him in Tango lessons, and pestering me about Bhutan. Now in the midst of this little essay, I will certainly be more attentive to these "opportunities". I don't know about the outcomes, but I do know that life will become that much richer for taking a risk or two. MKG

From Turmoil to Tranquility

One of our guiding hopes in these little essays is to replace the way we view aging in terms of what we lose with a focus on what we gain. Among the gains we have reported in the past is a generalized increase with age in feelings of emotional well-being. Replacing the gut wrenching agonies of the earlier years are feelings of greater tranquility. One knows how it goes and has a more balanced understanding of life and its ups and downs. Researchers Michaela Riediger and Alexandra Freund now add a new dimension to the earlier work. Daily life in the adult world is often one of breathless turmoil. It is not simply that one so often feels "behind" in one's work, but there is never time enough to care for family and friends, for attending to one's personal needs, or repair and upkeep of one's living place or possessions. And this is to say nothing of planning for a vacation or one's financial or professional future. The personal investments are enormous, and we are spread all too thin. There is a sense of agonizing unrest that accompanies virtually all one's activities. Time and effort devoted to one need, desire, or ideal is always at the cost of something else. Catching up on work is often at the expense of family; time with family It is here that the research of Riediger and Freund is reassuring. In two studies, with over 140 participants ranging in age from 20–70 years of age, the researchers took measures of motivational conflict (i.e. the feeling that one wants to or should be doing something else in a given situation). As both studies demonstrated, such conflicts tend to disappear with increasing years. Possibly there are fewer tasks or commitments as one ages and more time available.

Maybe one has learned to move more gracefully and confidently through a multiplicity of motivational goals. These researchers also took measures of emotional well-being. Similar to preceding studies, these measures also showed increases in feelings of well-being with age.

And, most significantly, the increase in feelings of well-being were correlated with reductions in motivational conflict. So, for our younger readers, there is a lightness of being ahead.

Reference: Riediger, M. and Freund, A.M. (2008). Me against myself: Motivational conflicts and emotional development in adulthood. *Psychology and Aging, 23,* 479-494.

The Enchantment of Everyday Life

A friend of ours is approaching her 90th birthday, and just embarked on a project to redecorate her living room. She wants the room painted a different color, new furniture, pictures to match the décor, and more. Such decoration is scarcely required; her present living room is quite nice. Is she being irrational, then, just failing in her advanced age to accept the facts of life? On the contrary. As we see it, this flight of fantasy makes a real contribution to her well-being. She is looking beyond the ordinary and acceptable to create a space that adds a degree of sparkle to everyday life. To continue on the routinely functional path is secure enough, but unremarkable and uninteresting. It is the imagined world of the not yet real that generates the zest for living.

One might say that our friend is engaging in what Morris Berman once called the enchantment of the world. There is something about "the plain facts" that drains life of significance. It is only when we inject value into something that it begins to matter. Thus, if life is to be engaging, inviting, and compelling, we need to add enchantment to the ordinary.

What would this mean in practice? The possibilities are endless. But we have been struck especially by the ways in which some people can add glow to otherwise ordinary occasions. By adding a flower to the breakfast table, calling distant friends on their birthdays, saving a chocolate for just the right moment, setting out for a walk in a beautiful place, playing favorite music while preparing dinner, wearing a robe that feels especially good, choosing a special film to share, or lighting an incense stick at bedtime, we enchant our worlds.

Reference: Berman, M. (1981). *The Re-enchantment of the World*. Ithaca, NY: Cornell University Press.

IV. SKILLS IN ACTION

Buddhist Practices For All Seasons

The two of us have spent many hours helping to bring into print a new book, *Horizons in Buddhist Psychology*. This work has been especially inspiring for us, as it has pointed to significant ways in which Buddhist practices can contribute to positive aging. For one, they can expand appreciation for the daily worlds we live in, and prevent these worlds from becoming commonplace and boring. Practices of "mindfulness"—or the training of attention—are a gateway to living in the here and now, appreciating more deeply and fully what is before us at the moment. Buddhist practitioners encourage sharp focusing on details of sight, sound, taste, and touch. All of your attention is directed to one small bit of the world, and you see it in new and captivating ways. As a Buddhist monk advised, "You may find an entire universe in a drop of dew."

Buddhist practices can also lift stress. Normal life will not let us escape difficult or anguished times, and the challenge is how to respond with composure, balance and clarity. Here the most helpful practice is meditation. Effective meditation does not require hours of training and quietude. With a little guidance, one can learn meditative techniques that require only a few minutes and that allow you to step outside the stress and strain of everyday experience, and to return with a fresh outlook. Here we have found breathing exercises particularly useful.

These practices also carry with them promising attitudes toward life. For one, there is a close connection between the practices and a sense of compassion toward others. Buddhist practices often deepen one's sense of connection to all other creatures, and invite more caring relationships. As well, there is no attempt in the Buddhist tradition to treat our states of fear, tension or anguish as pathological. People are not categorized in terms of depression, traumatic stress, attention deficit and the like. To engage in practices of focused attention and meditation enables us to move more effectively and positively in a world where suffering is simply a normal part of life. We find wonderful potential here.

Reference: Kwee, M., Gergen, K.J. and Koshikawa, F. (2006). *Horizons in Buddhist Psychology*. Chagrin Falls, OH: Taos Institute Publications. (www.taospub.net)

Exploring Time, Enriching Life

A common maxim, offered by sages from many times and places, is to live in the moment, one day at a time. There is much to be said for this advice, but in our view, it is limited. There are also riches to be derived from immersing oneself in times past, and too, thinking creatively about the future. Engaging in all three dimensions of time—present, past, future—offers great riches. Consider for a moment the upward limits of "living in the present." We were both struck by a poem entitled "A Maxim" by Carl Dennis published in the *New Yorker*. Dennis notes that it was Marcus Aurelius who first gets credit for the injunction to "live each day as if it might be the last." However, as the poem wryly suggests, this might entail working on one's will in the morning, and saying goodbye to dear ones the rest of the day. After a while, the poet notes, most people would try desperately to avoid you. Rather, he suggests that we take an hour each day to pay our bills, forgive someone, or write a letter of thanks or apology. He ends by suggesting that one think of the future:

"No shame in a ticket to a concert seven months off,
Or, better yet, two tickets, as if you were hoping
To meet by then someone who'd love to join you,
Two seats near the front so you catch each note."

Yet, there are untold riches to be derived from looking backward as well. As theologian Soren Kierkegaard once wrote, "Life can only be understood backwards." It is in the process of reminiscing that we come to understand our lives. Indeed, in the current "life review" movement, much is made of sharing stories from the past with others, of bringing back into public focus not only the many selves one has lived—including adventures and mishaps—but as well the many loved ones who have helped us to find meaning in our lives. In sum, the best advice seems to be: move within all registers of time—present, past, and future—and from them draw rich resources for living.

In My 75th Year

We want to share a letter from Sara, a dear friend from California. Her husband asked her to write an essay on what it is like to be 75 years old, This may sound strange, but he teaches a college course on lifespan development, and thought his students might like to learn first-hand about aging. As Sara told us, her task was to write about, "How do I grow old gracefully? Or how have I coped with things like: retirement and downsizing; losing friends, family, and affiliations; inevitable physical decline; setting new goals when circumstances change, or dropping whatever you must drop. And what wisdom is there in all this "growing old", or as some optimists say, "growing better"?

Sara wrote at length about the problems she confronted in growing older. However, upon reflection, she also found that she had substantial resources for living a full and fulfilling life. Among other things, she wrote of the importance to her of remaining "myself through changes (biological and social)." In effect, she did not let age become her identity. She also counted as resources her "even temperament; being financially practical, living 'green'; being continuously considerate and helping friends." The latter two resources resonated well with research that shows the importance of relationships for one's continued well-being.

Sara also wrote of the particular resolves that helped her most in confronting some of the challenges of aging. In particular, she stressed:

- Watching my diet. Fitness is more important than body fat.

- Mindful Attention, Focus, Aesthetic appreciation,

- Working on my memory—Learning new tasks.

- Continuing education, water color, starting book group & clay group, learning the computer

- Volunteering for community service.

- Teaching reading to poor kids; working for museum

- Keeping active; Health club; yoga; fix up home and garden, making decisions

- Life Review, Self-reflection; writing group; hopefully gaining perspective & wisdom.

We thank you, Sara, for sharing your insights.

A Wild and Precious Life

The poet Mary Oliver once wrote, *"Tell me, what will you do with your one wild and precious life?* In approaching the later years of life it has special significance. It doesn't ask us to look back and evaluate what we have done. We can scarcely change the past in any case. What it does ask, is "what comes next." Rather than treating the past as fundamentally the end of significant living, it suggests that today is the first day of the rest of our lives. There may be amazing worlds open to us, if we search with optimism and flexibility. As much research reports, we gain in health, energetic engagement and a sense of well-being if we can approach the future with a sense of positive anticipation. These don't have to be big plans for adventure. Ideally no hour should go by in which we cannot find a little gem of wisdom, of humor, or love, and doing something one likes. If it isn't right there beside us, then we might stretch our arms a bit to find it. There is always a piece of chocolate to eat, a hug to share, a thank-you note to write, a phone call to a friend, an instrument to play, a book to open, a sweater to knit, a child to play with, a new recipe to try, a neighbor to visit, or a hammock to swing in.

There are bigger possibilities. Today I listened to a man in a shop talk about his mother. "She had rented a house in the Alps in Austria and was taking a hiking trip. She is trying to find her life again. My Dad died this year, and this is what she's doing to start over. When I was a baby my folks were tour guides for teenagers, traveling by bus around Europe. I went on my first trip to France when I was 2 weeks old. Then they stopped touring so they could raise a family and stay in one place for a while. I guess my Mom is trying to jump start her life again, going back to where they left off. This is the first time she's ever been in Austria, so I guess she is starting something new as well. She's not wasting any time discovering herself again." Now that's a wild and precious possibility! MKG

Needed: Category Busters

There were the heroes of gang busters and ghost busters, and now we need a new variety of hero: the category buster. By this we mean people who challenge the common attempt to describe and explain us in

terms of set categories. Recently an Irish therapist colleague argued strongly against understanding clients in terms of diagnostic categories. She
was especially concerned with people who are called "disabled" because
of the effects of this category on their lives. Once they accepted the label
into their lives, they began to shape their lives around it. In a sense, they
imprisoned themselves. The same is true of such categories as "aging" and
"old." It is not only that such labels suggest constraints over how we may
behave, they also reduce our sense of who we are. Some time ago a friend
at a party introduced another woman, as "Julie, a cancer survivor." Julie
recoiled at this definition of herself because it shoved all the other aspects
of her identity into the shadows of a diagnosis.

Such thoughts were magnified by the front cover of the *New York
Times Magazine*, some years ago, which featured a New York Yankee
baseball player with a candle on his helmet, standing on a birthday cake.
The caption read, "Derek Jeter turns 37, an age that, for a professional
athlete, is nothing to celebrate." Inside, a long article featured statistics on
the decline of aging athletes. However, less than a month later the short-
stop climbed into the record books when he reached 3,000 hits, an achievement that is rare in baseball history. Further, this hit was a home run; the
fans were delirious. Jeter's category defying behavior was equaled as well
by two women tennis players in the recent finals of the French Open. Both
women—Na Li from China and Francesca Schiavone from Italy—were
hovering in their 30s, an age when most women tennis players are considered well past their supposed prime. Now, however, we must celebrate
the category busters in their later years. These are the heroes among us
who disregard the cultural expectations, who refuse to be constrained
by categories. They reject the common phrase "I am too old to ..." flirt,
go dancing, enter the contest, buy a sports car, have my teeth fixed, visit
Egypt, learn Spanish, go white water rafting, etc. They are more like our
friend who survived cancer to take up running at the age of 50, and who at
the age of 70 is an award winning distance runner. These are the new he-

roes; they challenge the common stereotypes and in doing so contribute to lasting cultural changes. They also invite us all to think freshly about what is possible in our own lives.

The Call to Creativity

The greater part of adult life is occupied with functional duties. We confront the problems of work, of raising children, keeping up a household, balancing budgets, and so on. Our sense of worth is often linked to how well we can meet these challenges and move forward. As many people facing retirement agonize, "If I am not achieving anything, what value do I have?" Yet, as we enter a period of life in which functional duties are no longer so demanding, there is also reason to challenge the idea that one must earn one's worth. Certainly as children we did not feel this way, and the times of greatest joy were often those in which we were engaged in creative play. Is there wisdom to be found in returning to such activity?

This possibility was recently brought home to us by a dinner companion, Christina Robertson. Christina had just completed her PhD dissertation with Saybrook Graduate School on the topic of creativity and aging. As she enthusiastically described, she had enrolled in her study 20 people over the age of 65 who were intensively engaged in creative activity—either by profession or avocation. (Such activities included painting, writing, composing poetry, choral singing, and making crafts). Through intensive interviews and various standardized measures Christina found compelling evidence that the engagement in creative activity had lent a strong meaning to their lives; it gave them joy and a sense of fulfillment. Many also felt that such activity helped them through the challenges of aging. They didn't dwell so much on the negatives, and they felt more as if they could "go with the flow" of change. And many felt that their creative work inspired their sense of spirituality and a greater acceptance of death.

As we have found, the call to creativity is reaching increasing numbers of elders. We have seen retired friends who have begun piano lessons, writing poetry, and working on a novel. Two friends, who were no more than shutter-bugs during their professional careers, are now exhibiting their photographic work. Another has just given a magnificent organ concert to a large community gathering. Still others, in less noticeable but no less creative ways, are exploring the art of Indian cooking, raising honeybees, and growing spectacular flowers. And for those who have not heeded the call to creativity on their own, there are numerous organization now offering extensive programs for elders. (See www.creativeaging.org) One award winning initiative, carried out by the New Courtland Elder Services in Philadelphia, offers opportunities to more than 1,300 frail elders to work in animated video, mixed media, photography, quilt making, mosaic murals, doll-making and intergenerational choirs. Not only have they found that such engagement reduces loneliness, helplessness and boredom, but the work of these elders has led to exhibits and celebrations.

In our quieter moments we reflect: why should we think of creativity as confined to particular activities, such as art, dance, gardening, and the like? Could we not think of moving through each day as an art form, much like jazz improvisation, juxtaposing events and activities in such a way that a harmonious and satisfying whole results?

Reference: Robertson, Christina (2005) Creativity and aging: A grounded theory study of creative older individuals. Unpublished PhD dissertation, Saybrook Graduate School and Research Center.

The Unsung Heroes

There is a popular slogan making the rounds, "Old Age is Not for Sissies." And to be sure, with increased threats to health and life, the loss of spouses and friends, and the like, it is easy to understand why. However, one feeling that has often swept us up is sheer admiration for the way so many older people meet these harrowing challenges and continue to live lives of significance. We have now come to feel that they constitute a class of heroes, displaying ingenuity, determination, and bold resistance to the challenges of time. A recent political election offered up one story we want to share: Ray was nearing his 75th birthday. He was a long way from home, visiting his grandchildren, a new baby and a 3-year-old boy. While eating his breakfast with his grandson one morning, he suddenly collapsed and fell to the floor. The boy cried out, "Grandpa, what are you doing?" The boy's father heard him, and rushed to the kitchen. Ray was unconscious and apparently dying of a heart attack. With extensive CPR and the medics' repeated attempts with a defibrillator, Ray finally began to breathe. In the hospital he slowly began to recover. With continuing need for care, including pain relief for his 10 broken ribs from the paramedics' treatments, he was released a week later. With only a 5% survival rate for this kind of episode, the word "miracle" was whispered among the family.

With his wife , Ray was finally able to fly home to Philadelphia. Knowing about his brush with death, we were shocked when two days later, we ran into him making phone calls in a political campaign head-quarters! He had volunteered to get out the vote for the elections, and he didn't want to let the people counting on him down. Ray is not alone in his heroism; he speaks for so many others, but in a very loud and inspiring voice.

Respite and Renewal

A close friend recently complained to me about eating Sunday dinner at her mother-in-law's home. The mother-in-law was in her mid-80s, and as my friend described these visits, the dishes were not clean, there were moldy foods in the refrigerator, the carpets smelled of cat urine, the furniture was dusty, and the furnishings were depressingly dingy and in disrepair. I must admit this rang a bell for me. Ken and I have lived in our home for over 30 years. Our surroundings give us tranquility and pleasure. Each stick of furniture, each picture, and every decorative item is safe in its usual place, and a constant contributor to meaningful memories. There is history here, and a sense of our place in the world. At the same time, each beloved piece is gathering dust, disintegrating and absorbing the knocks of many years of use.

I thus decided to play a mental game with myself. I imagined myself as my daughter-in-law, walking through our house. With her eyes I began to see how the refrigerator really does need a thorough cleaning. The living room chair needs repair, as do three dining room chairs. The hall carpet is worn, there is dust on the picture frames, a cobweb in the hall corner, the front door is grimy and so on. What is it like for family and friends to visit? The result of this game is that I enlisted Ken's services in doing some major upgrading. And these efforts have been revealing. We have come to re-appreciate the furnishings, renewed memories, see paintings with fresh eyes, and spot the need for new appliances. We are energized!

In my view there is an important message here. As we grow older our surrounds can increasingly provide nurturing and enriching support—safety, tranquility, and meaning. Yet, these joys must also be balanced with a significant investment in renewal. The renewal of the surrounds is vitalizing and extends our consciousness both into the past and into the future. And perhaps family and friends will be happier too! MKG

Doing New Things Together

t is common to view childhood as the major phase of development—
when we learn to walk, to speak, and relate to others. And then there are
the years of formal education where acquire our basic knowledge of the
world. The so-called middle years of adulthood are those in which we use
our knowledge and sharpen the skills relevant to one's life pursuits. Then,
as the story goes, people just retire and grow older. No new skills are
required, and in fact, few demands are made on those they have acquired;
slowly they slip away. This is not only a depressing picture of aging, it is
wholly misleading. Older life is a major period of development, and its
rewards may eclipse any previous period of life. If aging is to be a positive

period of growth, new and important skills are required.

How is this so? Here it is useful to make a rough distinction between two general kinds of skills, those that expand the potentials of living and those that enable us to live with loss. In terms of expansion, think here of the child's learning to walk, ride a bicycle, or read. Each of these skills opens new vistas of possibility; life is enriched. In the case of loss, consider the way in which children must learn to give up their mother's breast, control their bowel movements, and curtail their emotional outbursts. And so it is with the elder years. Although rarely in the limelight, there are skills that can open new spaces of enrichment, and those essential in coping with loss.

Let's just focus here on one particular skill of enrichment, namely the skill of rediscovery. We recently spoke with an acquaintance who complained that his wife had become boring and indifferent. Why, he wondered, must he spend the rest of his life with someone who was not at all like the girl to whom he made his vows some decades earlier? His complaints also suggested why the divorce rates of people over 60 have been increasing of late. Obviously his spouse is not the same person, nor is he, nor are their children or friends, and so on. Particularly in families with a strong division of labor or with two careers, spouses or partners may scarcely notice changes in each other until retirement. With no one else around, and time to be together, suddenly one may confront a seeming stranger. The challenge then is rediscovery. What are the possibly hidden potentials of the other, the self, and the relational dance that can now blossom? There is no easy answer to this question, but promisingly, there may be many possible answers. Here are a few that have emerged from our conversations with each other and our friends:

- Seek out new contexts of relating: travel, sports, hiking, theater. Explore new relational activities: massage, cooking, gardening. Expand personal hobbies to include the other: golf, bridge, fishing.

- Re-explore the past together, with a focus on what has been nourishing. Explore the activities you once liked to do together, but which were abandoned.

- Allow your partner time and space for individual development and exploration, and encourage a later sharing.

- Be on the lookout for contexts in which you can pleasantly surprise the other.

We conclude by pointing out that we have learned a lot about these skills by talking with our friends. It is largely through our relationships that we continue to gain capacities.

Life Beyond Achievement

A Little League baseball team from our area recently had a chance to win the national finals. In the end they lost, but when they returned home they were treated to a hero's parade. I smiled with appreciation… but then a pause. After all, how many little league teams had competed and lost? And at what a young age all these kids began to worry about winning and losing…and mostly losing. Of course, they also have such worries in school where performance evaluation is an everyday concern. "How well will I do; how good am I; where do I stand in comparison to others?" Then, we leave school only to face a new set of hoops: "How well will I perform at my job; how good am I; how much money will I earn; am I a good enough parent; are my children living up to their abilities?" From early years to retirement, it's all about measuring up. Of course, the good word for all this is "achievement," and achievement can be fun—especially if you are a success! But there is always the pressure, the doubt, and the next day's challenge. More importantly, when we spend our lives trying to jump over hurdles, we begin to see life this way. We begin to ask, "Where is the next goal; what should I be accomplishing today?" We slowly forget how it is to live without climbing the next mountain.

When I was young the neighborhood kids would get together and play…anything and everything we could think of. We made up games, built a fort in the woods, ran a magic show, threw snowballs, played doctor…We didn't set out to accomplish anything; we would just play for the fun of it. I think now that if there had been a little league team, were observed by a coach and parents, and winning was the point, we would not have been "playing". We would have been achieving! We would play in order to win…not just for the creative fun of it. Our outdoor life would have become dutiful, not free. One of the joys of living long enough is that we can again, much more fully, tune into the process of living. We can take a walk—not to get someplace, but to enjoy the scenery or a passing conversation. We can jog or ride a bike, not as a means of training, but for the enjoyment of the movement. We can paint, cook, do some woodworking, go canoeing, write poetry, build some furniture, read a book, have a conversation, or work in the garden—not to accomplish some goal—but for the sheer pleasure of doing these things. Sure, there can be good results of our efforts. But now it's the process that counts; any accomplishment is just frosting on the cake. As Henry Miller once said, "The moment one gives full attention to anything, even a blade of grass, it becomes a mysterious, awesome, indescribably magnificent world in itself." This is fully living within the process. KJG

The Third Age as the Creative Age

To us, the phrase "third age" usually refers to the later years of life. But it says nothing about these years. We propose to define it as "the creative age." This conclusion was prompted by a recent critique in the *Baltimore Sun*. As Andrew L. Yarrow, a professor of history at American University, wrote, "Retiring when you're still in good health isn't just wrong, it's profoundly selfish and unpatriotic…Dropping out of the workforce while still in one's prime means ending one's contributions to America's strength, mortgaging our children's and grandchildren's future and leeching trillions of taxpayer dollars from the economy… If millions of Americans worked until age 67 instead of 62…[they] would increase national output and personal wealth and keep the labor force at a healthy level."

These were strong words, but they were met with some fierce rebuttals. As one reader wrote, "How times change! It used to be that people were encouraged to retire as soon as they reached the statutory age so as to 'get out of the way' of younger workers… Now we're 'unpatriotic' if, after slogging away in the work force for 40 or 50 years, we want to devote our remaining years of good health to traveling or pursuing our hobbies … give me a break!!" Another was more indignant, "I had to laugh after reading Andy Yarrow's plea to keep the shoulder to the wheel until age 65 or longer. He's got a cushy University job while the rest of us blue collar types work in physically punishing jobs. He is the classic case of an egghead who doesn't even know where eggs come from…an older person who wants to get the hell out of the rat-race should be able to do so when they want to." However, one further comment seemed most compelling, "Seniors can become extremely productive without having to associate with the corporate lifestyle. We need to see a paradigm shift for seniors from basically consumption efforts to more creative and productive projects. This new direction can always be combined with family, leisure, or any 'other' pleasurable retirement activities."

With this comment, the image of the creative age becomes clearer. Provided one has the financial security, the years following a full-blown career offer an unprecedented period in which one can envision, explore, and create a richly fulfilling lifestyle. As survey research indicates, the majority of those working in the private sector would prefer work that more directly benefits society. The creative age offers just such possibilities.

As it now stands, those in the creative age already contribute enormously to the well-being of their children, grandchildren, and their communities. And, as we see it, exploring the world, developing new skills, meeting new challenges, savoring these joys, and sharing our enthusiasm with those around us, is an ideal scenario for the "creative age."

"What counts most with colors are relationships," Matisse thought.

Reconstruction as Resource

We often encounter headlines warning of the hazards accompanying a long life—physical impairments, loss of memory, slackening abilities, the death of friends, and the like. But it's also important to consider our common definitions of "hazard." A broken leg is not simply a "painful setback." That is a common way to define it, but not the only way. What if it could be defined as "an opportunity to read some novels that I never had time for," or to "invite my children or grandchildren in for conversations for which we were always too busy"? What had been a reason for grimacing now becomes an inviting opportunity. As we see it, the capacity for redefining our condition is one of life's major resources.

This conclusion was vividly illustrated by two experiences of recent weeks. On the lighter side, we were fortunate enough to visit New York City's Museum of Modern Art, and see a major exhibit of Matisse's famous cut-outs. But one of the most interesting things about this blazing array of works was its origins. In his early 70's Matisse's eyesight was failing, and after surgery for cancer he was confined to a wheelchair. His days as a skilled painter were over. Rather than retiring from the scene, however, Matisse found that he could cut pieces of colored paper into shapes, and with the help on an assistant, arrange the shapes into collages. In the 14 years that followed, hundreds of works were produced. These became some of the most admired and influential works of his entire career. Effectively, Matisse had achieved a radical reconstruction. The world is all the richer as a result.

Closer to home, we were saddened to learn of the death of one of Ken's college classmates Carter Volz. The story he left behind, however, stands as a beacon for us all. Carter went on from Yale to receive an MBA, and to advance swiftly up the ranks in the corporate world. Within 20 years he became the Vice President of one of America's top corporations. Then tragedy struck.

Carter was mugged on a street in New York and left for dead. He did survive, but with serious brain damage, he was no longer able to hold his executive position. His time became devoted to recovery. It was during rehabilitation that he discovered Reiki, a Buddhist inspired form of hands-on healing. So effective did he find this form of therapy that he began to learn the skill. Over time he became a Master, and apprenticed many students. Further, in the last twenty years of his life, he went on to write books on Reiki, Jungian analysis, grief, and self-healing. He reconstructed his life, with positive consequences for himself, as well as the world.

The lives of these two men underscore the enormous potentials residing in our capacities for reconstructing meaning. In exploring "new ways of seeing things," we open new ways of being. As we grow older, this may be the key resource for well-being.

V. RELATIONSHIPS: THE VITAL SOURCE

Gifts and the Valuing Process

t is currently the season in which giving and receiving objects takes on special importance. At the same time, most of us are wary of the materialism that creeps into the holiday season. Indeed most of us hope that it is not the gift but "the sentiment that counts." And we often make special efforts to insure that our care and love are symbolized in our gifts. Yet, regardless of our efforts, over time the symbolic value of the gift is often lost. Within months—sometimes even days—the giver is separated from the gift. The gift itself becomes but another addition to the inventory of possessions.

As we grow older we often surround ourselves with objects that once had symbolic value—mementos of our travels, photographs, trophies, and so on. At times, we may even view our material possessions—a house, an automobile, a wristwatch—as symbols of valued accomplishments. Yet, just as with the gifts of the season, over time the significance is often separated from the object. The object is supposed to have value, but we no longer find it there. The object is there, inert, sometimes gathering dust, and so often "the thrill is gone."

Drawing from much of the research we have reported in this newsletter over the last year, we propose that the key ingredient to sustaining value in all that surrounds us is the valuing process itself. The objects cannot themselves sustain their significance. Rather, from the very beginning the source of their value was located in our relationships. For example, a winner's trophy has significance for us only because at some point we joined in with others to create the value of success at a particular activity. Outside these relationships the trophy is relatively meaningless. (And so it is that after our demise our children will willingly sell objects of great emotional significance to us without any sense of loss.)

Invited, then, is a nurturing of those relationships in which value is created. Objects may come and go, but our relationships may continuously renew and reinforce the value we find in the world about us. It is a good season for celebrating relationships. In doing so we contribute to the very possibility of celebration itself.

Relational Life Review

Older people are often encouraged to engage in a life review, that is, to thoughtfully explore the details of their lives as a whole, to put together the "story of my life." There are groups for producing such memoirs, and younger family members are encouraged to interview their elder "before it is too late." By engaging in this process with an appreciative eye, one not only derives pleasure, but an enhanced sense of meaning and of peace. Life reviews focus on the self, as the center of activity. We try to discover "what happened to me, what I felt, decided, or thought…" Although the life review is a popular genre, the subject is very narrow. Time after time, national surveys indicate that the most important or valued aspects of people's lives are their relationships. So, we ask, what about laying aside the "story of *my* life," for a while, and instead review the *story of the relationships* of which I have been a part? What could we learn; how would this expand our consciousness or appreciation?

The two of us have played with this idea for some time, in one case trying our hand at a "duography," or a biography of our coupleship. We now find it illuminating to think back on the history of various other relationships in which we have participated. For example, what do we recall about early family life? Rather than thinking of "what happened to me," one might ponder what happened to my family over time, the relationship of father, mother, and siblings, and how we functioned together—for both good and ill. Here we begin, for example, to think of the economic struggles of our parents and their sacrifices for us, along with the way we brought them pleasure…and a bit of pain! We begin to appreciate the way our mothers seemed to hold us all together, and how, after her death, our relations with our brothers and sisters changed. And we also think of friendship relationships, some now inactive, some enduring. We don't ask in this case, "what did I get from this," but, for example, "how did *we* flourish so well," and "what joy did we create together?" And of course, there are the teams in which we have participated, the clubs, and the communities. All add significant layers to our understanding and appreciation.

Relations have a life of their own; we can participate, but like a lively conversation or a dance, the directions they take are born in the interaction. As we grow older, we need to explore the dynamics of these relationships, appreciate the dimensions they have added to the lives of the participants, including ourselves, and relish these sources of meaning and inspiration.

Meditations on Relational Fire

I t was a cold, grey and rainy day in mid-December. I awoke early, and slowly plodded my way to the kitchen. The house was dark, and no life was stirring. I looked out on the colorless landscape, much as it had been the previous day. And the day before that. Slowly I found myself asking questions I otherwise like to avoid: Where do I begin this day, and why? What is worth doing; how and why should I "light the fire" of the day? Nothing seems intrinsically significant, even my life itself. The questions moved me to meditate, "Well, Mary would love a coffee when she wakes," "Paul is waiting anxiously for my comments on his paper." "Michael was really hoping we could pick up our grandson from school today." "Maggie was hoping we would come to dinner." Slowly I began to realize that almost all the reasons for lighting the fire of the day were lodged in my relationships. Typically these were also relations of love, care, and respect.

Even when I thought about motivational sources that seemed "mine alone," they had a relational source. I love to write, but isn't it always with an appreciative audience in mind? I go out of my way for delicious food, but could not imagine eating it alone. And didn't I acquire my love for art and music from others' enthusiasms?

I then began to ponder the 27 victims of a school shooting in Newtown, Connecticut. What could possibly move a young man to murder all these innocent children? As the facts of his life began to emerge, a familiar pattern began to form: he was a loner, without friends, without organizational ties, and with alienated family relations. There were none of the relational connectors that would create the value of others, the importance of nurturing the process of relating. And indeed, without these connections there was reason for animosity toward those cozy bands that "abandoned" him, cast him out of the halls of meaning making.

There are important implications here for aging. Everywhere there is evidence pointing to increased depression and suicide in aging populations. Why should one go on living when each day is effectively "cold, dark, and rainy?" As one ages, there is typically a reduction in one's relational life. As my grandmother remarked when approaching her hundredth birthday, none of her friends remained alive. For the aging individual, the challenge then is to devote special attention to nurturing and sustaining one's relations. Go the extra mile, even when inconvenient. Further, do not rely on your existing network of relations alone. Seek ways to expand the arena of connection, whether face to face or electronically. There are also policy implications. Where the individual needs and capacities of older people have typically been foremost in planning, more attention should be paid to satisfying the relational needs of people, old or young. With vital relationships, there are vital beings. KJG

Lighting the Fire of Relationships

It is a special privilege to be allowed to share an inspiring story sent to us by the Danish translator of the *Positive Aging Newsletter*, Geert Mork:

In January 2013 I was sitting in a small wooden house next to the sea, alone, with nothing but snow around me. 10 miles to the nearest town— and no one to make coffee in the mornings. Life wasn't showing me its most smiling face those days.

At that moment one of the most important emails in my life showed up in my mailbox: the *Positive Aging Newsletter* no. 77. Ken talked about waking up in the morning in a cold and colorless landscape—pretty much like my own experience that very morning. And Ken—your beautiful story about motivational sources in our lives always having a relational source, touched me deeply. Just one year earlier me and my wife divorced after 35 years together, and I was slowly losing relations in my life...

That morning in January I suddenly realized that my focus on relations had been much too weak for many years. A couple of months later I was turning 60, and I started to think this as a unique opportunity to make some important changes in my life. I sent out invitations to a party to people I hadn't talked to for years but who used to be good friends in earlier years. I contacted family members I hadn't seen for 15 years—and invited them too. And they all showed up in April to celebrate, and really made some warm and loving days, recreating some important relations in my and their lives. And the best part of it was that almost everybody started talking about the importance of relations and the importance of not forgetting each other, which has now led to several more meetings during the spring and summer. Life started to show its most smiling face again :- -)

What I also want to share with you is this: in February I received an invitation to celebrate the 40-years high school anniversary. Normally I wouldn't respond to this. I did not participate in either the 10-year or the 25 year anniversary. But Ken´s commentary made me think differently. I accepted the invitation, and actually became one of the members in the planning-committee. And during the planning meetings during the spring an old appreciation of the most beautiful girl in the high school slowly grew again.

Thanks to your comment in your newsletter my whole life has changed dramatically. From being concerned about life and future to becoming aware of all the love and good things in life, based on old and new caring and close relations.

Altruism: Lessons for the New Aging

There is great pleasure in helping others. But the joys of helping turn sour when others need assistance—we are too tired to stand in a bus, to carry heavy objects, to master complex situations, and so on. But do we want to be helped on such occasions? The issues are complex because receiving help may define us in certain ways. For women, it is especially complex because there is the tradition of chivalry in which help from a man is a complement. There is also the feminist view that such help sustains the traditional stereotype of strong men vs. weak women. And so it is that as we age, attempts to help us seem to cast us into the dustbin: "You are old!" Behind the smile of gratitude, we might painfully be asking, "Do I really look that old?" Sometimes it is annoying, as in the cartoon when the old lady tells the Scout, "But I didn't want to cross the street."

These issues came home for us recently when a younger couple from Asia came for a visit of several days. We are used to entertaining foreign visitors in our home, and as these scholars had a keen interest in our professional work, our altruistic intentions were high. Alas, theirs were too! As we tried to behave as gracious hosts, they carried out their cultural tradition by treating us as "revered elders." This tension was played out in many ways. After an hour's conversation, they felt we must be tired. They wakened early so that they could make breakfast for us; on their final day they announced that they wished to clean our house. We struggled to teach them that none of this was necessary; rather we wished to treat them as valued guests. We worked it out… It seems to us that a major challenge confronting the older and fitter generations of today is teaching the young when and where help is appreciated. They need to learn more about "the new aging," and the continuing strengths that can be enjoyed into the 90s. At the same time, we must also take into account the desires of the young to be helpful. When one's grown children want to host a family get-together, for example, one must learn to graciously accept the favor. It is a gift to them to express pleasure in their care of us. Times are changing, and we must be teachers as well as learners.

The Rise of Senior Capital

Robert Putnam's popular book, *Bowling Alone*, represented a painful lament at the loss of what is commonly called social capital. Social capital is represented, for one, in the network of local relations in which people are linked by a sense of trust and reciprocity. Such capital is critical to the well-being of local communities, for without the dedication of neighbors to each other—in terms of time, resources, solidarity, and care—the civic fiber is destroyed. People may reside close by, but there is no community. With the increase in two career families, distributed obligations, and travel demands—together with the lure of television, mobile communication, and the internet—social capital is in short supply.

As we see it, the expanding population of elders is a preeminent source for renewing social capital. We have already seen this in the activities of many of our friends. As one recent put it, "I feel my entire career has been devoted to the corporate rat race, and making gains for myself and my family; at this point I would like to give something back to society." He now devotes his efforts to the Board of a struggling college that serves African American students. Another friend served voluntarily well into his 80s as the mayor of a local community. A widow friend has taken an interest in schools and communities with inadequate libraries, and devotes her intelligence and pocketbook to their improvement. Another serves as a voluntary ombudsman representing prisoners at a local prison. And this is to say nothing of those who nurture grandchildren while parents are away, care for their neighbors' houses and pets when they are absent, serve on neighborhood watches, and run errands for the infirm.

There may be additional benefits for many of the folks. Research suggests that volunteering to help others not only brings with it feelings of fulfillment, but can expand one's friendship circle, and give one needed physical activity. All this contributes as well to good health. As the research reported below suggests, the more we reach out to support others, the better our health. At the same time, we are only beginning to tap into the huge resources available in the aging population. Research shows that only 23 percent of those 65 and older participate in any volunteer efforts. This is not for lack of desire on the elders' part. As a Harvard University report, *Reinventing Aging*, indicates, most seniors want to work with others, make use of their skills, and expand their knowledge. A further study by Temple University's Center for Intergenerational Learning reports that elders want to participate in meaningful activities (not stuffing envelopes), and they want organizations to provide respect and admiration for what they do, along with some concrete rewards (such as transportation or reimbursement for expenses.) In effect, if we wish to tap the enormous potential of Senior Capital, efforts must also be made to be more sensitive to their needs and appreciative of their dedication.

Meaning in Life

The two of us are in high spirits as we drive through the countryside, stopping at designated houses, to "get out the vote." We chat with each other about how important it is that our candidate be elected, and how worthwhile it is to sacrifice our normal routine to make even a small difference. And then, on election night, 2008, we join the millions who celebrate an election outcome that spells hope for the country and possibly for the world. These are weeks of high drama for us. Yet, it is at times like this that we come face to face with questions of value. What kind of world do we want; why is it worth making these sacrifices? The usual advice is to look inward; find within yourself what you truly value. Yet, when we consider the enthusiastic dedication of these election weeks, this traditional advice seems wrong-headed. For the two of us, the importance of the election was not born in some isolated region of the brain, but was kindled within our relationships. This was not private inspiration, but the result of spirited discussion with friends and colleagues. Is this same relational process not the origin of whatever joy we derive from our professional work? And in our private lives? Even in bearing children and raising them to adults, isn't the sense of fulfillment provided by a longstanding tradition that endows these activities with value? In effect, if the day is to be filled with a sense of excitement as opposed to boredom or depression, significant relationships are essential.

There are important implications here for the aging process. With retirement one often exits a network of work relationships; children abandon the nest; and there are deaths of the near and dear. All such losses may bring about a loss in life's meaning. This first suggests that we should nurture and cherish existing relationships. Taking our relationships for granted or letting them deteriorate through disuse or abuse is an invitation to ennui. Nor should we view the cast of significant others as firmly established somewhere along the path. Rather, as we grow older we should be ever open and inviting to new and life-giving connections. The same may be said for pastimes and hobbies. Exploring new vistas of interest can expand the sea of relationship. By nurturing and expanding relationships, the drama of life remains robust.

Small Talk as Daily Bread

had never liked small talk; for me, it seemed to be directionless chit-chat about nothing in particular. Invitations to small talk were everywhere, invited by neighbors, friends, guests, my assistant at the office. It was there at dinner parties, on train rides, and on planes—should I ever give an opening to the person sitting next to me to talk. My concerns were elsewhere—to the "important things in life," solving problems, making progress, and reaching goals. Those were matters truly worthy of conversation. I have now changed my mind about small talk. There is another story to be told about its value, and its special importance as we grow older.

For me the story began when I was giving a month of lectures at a university in St. Gallen, Switzerland. Because there was no guest-house for professors, I was quartered in the spacious apartment of an 86 year old widow. I didn't look forward to my tenure in the household, because Frau Ferlein seemed introverted and spoke only German. At the same time, I was trying to better my fluency in the language so a little conversation with her seemed a good idea. I began to notice, however, that as I asked her questions about her life, and intensely sought to comprehend her replies, a transformation began to take place. As I attended to her, her reticent voice acquired volume; her timidity gave way to humorous story telling. As the days went by, I too began to change. I found myself listening not to improve my language skills, but because she was simply fun to be with. I became animated by the exchanges, and by the end of two weeks we were rollicking good friends. At the end of my stay, parting was indeed sweet sorrow. When I returned to visit her the following year, her buoyant energy had sadly disappeared. Take away conversation and you take away life.

So, where lies the magic power of small talk? Consider this: Mary and I are taking a walk, and I casually say, "Hmm, seems to be clouding up." Now contrast two possible responses, the first just a simple "hmm" as she stares straight ahead. The second is an energetic, "Oh well, at least we won't be sunburned." With the first response, something in my world also turns grey. I trudge onward in silence. With the second, the clouds now gain a new and more positive meaning. I may even chuckle. And what's more, I myself take on significance. My step becomes lighter. For in her humorous response, Mary injects importance into the otherwise mundane.

My interest is heightened. She is also affirming my significance to her. I am brought into being as a person whose words—even if otherwise trivial—hold value. In small talk we give our worlds color and dimension, and we affirm each other's significance. Sometimes we also learn things we didn't know or didn't even know we wanted to know!

And so it is, as we grow older, as the ranks of our age-mates begin to thin, and the demands of working life are lessened, that we can appreciate anew the life-giving potentials of small talk. In the cheery greetings, a brief chat with neighbors, trading stories on the telephone, or sending small notes by email, text or mail, we animate the world about us. And in our daily lives with our partners, the small acts of appreciation, the attention we give to their well-being, the sympathetic gaze, or just the way we are energized when they enter the room, is significant. With small talk we affirm the significance of the realities we have created and enrich the world in which we live. KJG

Aging and Physical Attraction: A Dialogue

Recently a reader of our *Positive Aging Newsletter* wrote us about a very sensitive issue to many: aging and the loss of attractiveness. We include her message here, and Mary Gergen's reply:

READER: I am wondering if you have ever dealt with any fears around aging, particularly in terms of feeling a loss of attractiveness. If so, how did you deal with it? I have had an intense fear of aging since I was in my twenties (am now 58), and it seems to revolve around my fear of being old and unattractive. Though I do have a rich spiritual life, which includes a regular meditation practice, the fear remains and is, in fact, growing. And, of course, it sabotages my peace of mind.

MARY: I think we all become conscious as we age that we are becoming more and more invisible in terms of being physically attractive creatures. For some women it seems to be a blessing; for some, it was never important in the first place; but for many, it is experienced as you say, with fear and regret. The media and the social sciences collaborate in creating this negative situation. But there it is. I even wrote a journal article about 20 years ago called "Finished at 40" about the lack of interest in women as they matured. However, today, I think I would call it "Finished at 50" because 50 is the new 40. There has been a shift in what we think Old means. Still…

A few women I've known have remained quite alive in a sensual way into their late 70's. One of my friends, Adele, was a wonderful flirt at 99. In my view it seems primarily a matter of style, a way of being in the world, as to whether or not you are seen as attractive. I recall that Ken was absolutely intrigued at a dinner party one evening as he sat next to an artist well into her 80s. She had a way of being glamorous that transcended the specifics of her age. I think there is a great range in the ways of getting older, and there are models of aging that appeal to some more than others…I like the "Auntie Mame" idea…being rather unorthodox and free. Wearing what I want… doing what I want.

Letting my beauty be in my ways of being…and hoping people enjoy my presence, and appreciate my style.

To myself, I am still a beautiful woman… and so at times it is rather surprising to look into the mirror and see the older woman I have become. I suppose I might go to a plastic surgeon if I felt very strongly about it. Two of my best friends from college did so when they were 60. But I still feel that it is ultimately style over substance (in this case bodily) that counts. I know physically beautiful women who have no problem in attracting lovers, but they are so self-centered and critical that no one cares to share a life with them. (A former professor of mine once told me about his marriage to just such a woman, and he found it unbearable to be with someone who only thought about her own physical being. Later I met his second wife, who was an average looking woman who was above all charming, funny, and kind. He was devoted to her.)

There are two small thoughts I have found useful over the years. First, when I look back at early photos and begin to feel forlorn about my present state, I say to myself: If I look back in 10 years at the photos taken of me today, I will feel, "Oh, not bad looking." I suspect the same will happen when I look back ten years from now on photos of today. A second thought remains with me daily: people always seem to worry about the wrong things. It is life's surprises that usually bring the demons. So, perhaps we should not spend too much time on useless worries. It's better to count our blessings.

The Power of Conversation

In 2014 the two of us were in Nanjing, China, giving lectures. There we met a graduate student from Nanjing Normal University, Tian-fang Liu. Liu had been reading the Chinese translation of our Newsletter, and was eager to share her experience with us. Her story was touching, and had implications for us all. We are happy to pass on her story:

"About three months ago, I volunteered for a nursing home where I met Sha, a 94 year old woman. At my first visit, she was lying on her bed in a darkened room, like a wooden, lifeless puppet. Her face was tired, listless, and dull. When I started talking to her, she slurred in her native accent: 'Don't you know how old am I? I'm nine---ty... years...old...ol---d enough. I have lived long-----enough in the world, just waiting for approaching death. I am a worthless being, not needed anymore. That's why I live in this institution…I was abandoned by my three sons…I have nothing to do at all except wait for death.' At that moment, I was terribly sad, shocked…and then angry: Is this the kind of life women entering old age should deserve? They have sacrificed themselves to their family, children and society, and this is the return!!!

As a young graduate student, I have no power or money; perhaps the only resource I have is my education. After returning to the university, I started to search for research on positive aging, and to talk with my supervisor, colleagues and friends about this woman. As they suggested, it might be helpful to be curious about the woman's life. Ask questions, like how she was able to survive during the Second World War (She was 17 in 1937 when it began) and the Cultural Revolution from 1966 to 1976, to make her sense her good fortune. On my next visit I took their suggestions, and began to inquire into her life. She began to recount the hard times she had come through, but also sharing her stories of good fortune. In response, I also began to share some of my stories with her; I found her delighted to give me advice. As we conversed, I gradually found myself asking more questions and learning so much, for example, how to run a restaurant, what it's like to be married and become pregnant, how to raise and educate children, how to cook, and how to keep healthy. Perhaps she began to realize, just as I did, how capable, competent, skillful, experienced, and worthwhile she is. What a colorful life she had. When I left that day, she was smiling.

I continued to visit, and we continued to talk together. I began to see that she was tidying her bed and cleaning the room. She began to actively bathe herself rather than waiting for a social worker's help. Sometimes she goes for a little walk in the corridor, and even sings old songs to me when the time is right. Recently I discovered that every time I came, there was an empty chair beside her which, it seemed, was prepared for my arrival. The last time I was going to leave, she waved to me and said:" Do come to clean the chair next week!" Because a chair would be dusty if no one sits, this is a way we warmly invite people to visit us frequently.

So powerful are the effects of good conversation that I now seek ways to help Sha find other partners in the home. This has not been easy. But it is essential. As Sha complained to me: I now realize that talking is good, but if no one responds to you, how do you talk? Talk with yourself? Are you insane?" I shall also try to involve Sha's daughters and her sons and daughters-in-law; her children's visiting is her final dream.

Benefits of Aging: Giving and Receiving

We recently participated in a national conference on positive aging. One outstanding question that emerged during our workshop was: In contrast to all the talk about loss, what are the benefits of aging? One of the most interesting responses from our audience concerned the twin benefits of giving and receiving. As participants suggested, we spend most of our lives acquiring income, housing, goods, and so on. Yet, while a livelihood is essential, there is something empty about material self-seeking. The senior years provide an unparalleled opportunity to "give back." We are able to give more of our energies, ideas, and resources to our communities, and indeed, to the needy of the world. A grandmother in our midst told a wrenching story of her joy at bringing a grandchild back to life, after the little girl had suffered radical mistreatment from her father. A widower advocated "Saving the Earth" as a prime opportunity for older people, who have the wisdom, the resources, and the desire to preserve the planet for following generations.

On the receiving end, there were many stories, both funny and tender. One of the participants admitted that she played the "old lady" card from time to time, for example, taking the empty seat on the bus when several people might be standing. Most of us thought she well deserved to call in her credits, and to enjoy her status as an old lady. Another told the story of a bedridden woman who needed to receive care for the most basic needs of living, including help with toileting and feeding. Yet, despite her limitations, she expressed gratitude to her caretaker for every helpful act they provided. Those surrounding her felt blessed to have the opportunity to care for her. The later years have so much to offer, giving and receiving are only two of the salutary rewards.

VI. LONGEVITY AND MORTALITY

Skills in Reconstructing and Relinquishing

As we have proposed, aging well is an acquired skill. During every phase of life one must grapple with two important challenges: mastering the new and dealing with loss. Required in both cases are skills:

reconstructing and relinquishing. Here we want to focus on a particular case, our dear and recently deceased friend John. For us, he provided a stellar example of both these skills in action, and his life serves as an inspiration. John was a retired insurance broker, who had lived in the suburbs, fathered four children, and had been married for many years before a divorce. He was a Gary Cooper kind of guy—quiet, unassuming, friendly and conservative. John did have an interest in the arts, and it was during a gallery opening in Philadelphia that he met our longstanding artist friend, Deborah. In contrast to John, Deborah was animated, creative, and a Bohemian at heart. She lived in an artists' community with a lively group of colleagues. We were thus a little surprised when they took a liking to each other, and wondered how they would click as a couple. But click they did, and soon enough, John left the suburbs to take up residence with his new bride in her studio-home in the city. The reconstruction began. John had a longstanding interest in collecting old tools and cameras. Soon enough he began to take photography lessons, and with Deborah, to seek out interesting sites for his photo shoots. Within a few years he was exhibiting his work in various shows. He also took courses in welding, and began to find ways of using his old tools and cameras to create innovative statues. A statue he kept outside his studio door was made entirely of old cameras. As he developed these talents the public also began to take notice, and soon he was selling his works at various exhibits. The community of artists also accepted him into their midst, pleased to have his creative presence, as well as his managerial skills.

Alas, as life was expanding in all directions, John was also diagnosed with cancer. After several years of valiant resistance and times of recovery, his body began to lose the battle. The challenge now was that of relinquishing. John faced the inevitable with dignity, love for those about him, and an unstinting devotion to his art. For example, on his 80th birthday Deborah invited a dozen friends to a restaurant to celebrate. John had been undergoing radiation and chemotherapy, and his energies were low. As usual, he kept conversation about his illness to a minimum. It was treated as a rather minor sideline to the celebration of his birth. Deborah had asked that there be no gifts, but if we had an interesting metal piece to bring to John, that would be appreciated. There was more sculpting to do! Indeed, John continued to work in his studio until the week he died.

Zest and Zing: If You Ain't Got That Swing

We recently came across an interesting research study emphasizing the importance for longevity of being full of zest for life. Researchers studied the longevity of 320 Swedish octogenarians for 10 years, comparing those who had a high zest for life with those who did not score high on these indicators. Some of the questions used to test for "zest" were: "I am just as happy as when I was younger;" "These are the best years of my life"; and "I have gotten more breaks in life than most of the people I know." Quite dramatically, those who had the lowest Zest for Life scores had a risk of dying that was twice as high as those in the highest quartile. This was so, even when sex, age, number of serious illnesses, and frailty were taken into account. Researchers also controlled for social class, depressiveness, and social and cognitive functioning. Even when people had serious illnesses, their mortality was still more closely related to their zest for life than their disease prognosis.

Clearly having a zest for life seems to be a useful quality in having a long and satisfying life. Yet, we asked ourselves, what if one doesn't feel zestful and zingy? Does one just accept one's fate? Is it possible to create zesty feelings? We tried to come up with some ideas of how one could manufacture one's own bliss. These were some of our favorites:

1. Get enough good sleep, and eat properly as well. Make sure the body gets what it needs to operate at its personal best.

2. Focus on work and activity that are pleasing. If possible distance yourself from things you don't like doing. And if you can't distance yourself, try to think of the positive benefits of these activities.

3. Nurture your social networks—call your friends, invite them over, buy them little gifts, sing to them on their birthdays, and help them out when you can. Get rid of sour pusses—unless you are married to one. Then try other solutions.

4. Ice each day with some "frosting"… which means plan ahead for something exciting to look forward to, even if it's a favorite dish, a walk in the park, or calling your kids.

5. Focus your thoughts on the positive; find ways to let the negatives float by. Enjoy the beauty in the moment, as there is always something lovely to see, even in the most humble of surroundings.

6. Every day find ways to laugh, even at yourself.

7. Enjoy your pets and/or grandchildren; play and act silly with them.

8. Treat yourself to sensual pleasures (bubble baths, massages, whatever feels especially good to your body).

9. Give a gift of yourself to someone who appreciates it.

10. Learn something new—take a course, develop a skill, practice a new art, sing, play an instrument, teach something to others.

11. Exercise or dance or play games. Move as swiftly and gracefully as you can. Enjoy your body's capacities however you can.

12. Be forgetful of yourself. Be absorbed into the flux of life.

You may have other favorites. If so, share with others…the zest will multiply!

Reference: Satisfaction with Present Life Predicts Survival in Octogenarians by Tiina-Mari Lyra, Timo M. Tormakangas, Sanna Read, Taina Rantanen, & Stig Berg. *Journal of Gerontology: Psychological Sciences*, 2006, *61*, P319-326.

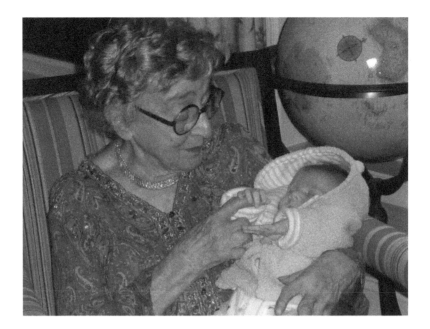

If Only I Were Younger

The view of aging as end-of-life decline is our enemy. We are left with a sense that the real opportunities are now past; it is too late to begin anything significant. And so we may be saddled with regret, and approach the future with lethargy. We are thus very grateful to a friend of ours, we call her "Mama," who gave us a present of a book on the occasion of her 90th birthday. She was right on target in thinking that we would want to share its message.

The book, *Granny D: You're Never Too Old to Raise a Little Hell* is the story of an 89 year old woman, Doris Haddock, who was beset by grief. Not only had her beloved husband of 62 years passed away, but so had her oldest best friend, Elizabeth. Rather than simply looking out at a bleak future, Granny D., as she is called, made a dramatic decision. As an honor to the departed, and to make a contribution to her country, she decided to walk across the country on her own. Granny D. was galled at how members of Congress were so often "bought" by the big corporations and money interests in the world and were no longer responsive to the average citizen. She wanted to do something about it.

She began her trek in California, and walked some ten miles a day. As Granny D. walked she collected a shifting coterie of family, friends and followers who helped her to face the desert heat, the traffic on narrow muddy roads, the snow filled mountain passes, and the moist green fields of the South and East. Ever determined, she cross-country skied on a canal path when the roads became too treacherous to walk. Along the way she was given hospitality by the rich and the poor; she attended African-American church services and rodeos, gave speeches in high schools, at county fairs and just about any place that people would listen. She was the star of many a parade and local celebration. She looked up influential lawmakers and tried to persuade them of her cause. At day's end, she would write in her journal, create her speeches, which are included in full length in the appendix, and unwrap the bandages on her feet and the steel corset that held her upright as she walked. Some days her emphysema and arthritis would get her down, but it never stopped her from her mission. She ended her walk in Washington, D.C. in time to see a campaign reform bill pass the House. She shared in the jubilation with Representatives Richard Gephardt, Christopher Shays and Mart Meehan, co-sponsors of the House version of the bill.

As she ended her mission she looked back with joy at her life. As she wrote, "I had come to look to my own beliefs and passions and had done something about them while there was yet time. In this, I had discovered what so many already know: that the art of your passion, embraced fully, redeems you from all the sins and shortcomings of a life." Granny D.'s message in brief is "It is never too late to do something about your dreams for yourself and your country."

Reference: *Granny D: You're Never Too Old to Raise a Little Hell* by Doris Haddock with Dennis Burke. New York: Villard, 2003

Positive Aging: Not all Smiley Faces

t is common for people to associate the word "positive" with light-heart-ed happiness. We have nothing against being joyful, but a "happy face" idea is not the vision of positive aging we prefer. For us the dimensions of positive aging are far richer and more emotionally complex. Our aim is to replace the "over the hill" metaphor of aging with one in which new life potentials are opened to us. Through aging, we may acquire, for example, a richer and more appreciative sense of ourselves in relationship to others and our environment. We may learn new skills, develop new loves, accomplish new things, and explore new places. Our appreciation for life's offerings may expand, our interests deepen, and our awe at the unknown be rekindled.

The significance of this view has been sharpened for us in our various workshops on positive aging. Often we confront our participants with the challenge of reconstruction. That is, we present them with the common stereotypes of decline and loss we carry with us through life and challenge them to imagine ways in which these "disasters of aging" may be viewed more positively. For example, in what ways can we possibly accept, and even appreciate, the so-called losses cease to simply be losses.

However, discussions become more difficult when it comes to the loss of spouses, partners, close friends, and, most especially one's children. How in the world can one find anything positive about the death of those one loves? Even the question seems abrasive. But this is again to equate the word "positive" with happy faces. The challenge here is to locate the kind of significance in these losses that remove them from the ledger of "loss is loss." Can we, for example, find within our sorrows a deeper appreciation for the lives of those no longer with us? Can we count the many ways in which they have enriched our lives and those of others?

Indeed, can we locate within our suffering an appreciation for the very fact that we suffer? Are such feelings not a tribute to those we have lost, and a signal of the depth of our relationship?

We often speak with our friends, Sharon and Bob Cottor, from Phoenix, Arizona about their grandson, Ryan. He was diagnosed in infancy with a fatal disease and has been living on borrowed time ever since. Amazingly, Ryan, who is pictured above, is now 12 years old.

Although there is always the potential to be saddened by this impending loss, Ryan's life has helped create a significant blessing for his community. The Ryan House (www.RyanHouse.org), named for him, is the creation of his family and now the greater Phoenix community, as a respite home for families with children with terminal illnesses. It has also become a place where children go with their loved ones to spend their last hours of life. The illness and impending death of this child have thus brought people closer and more caringly together, and helped families under stress to find respite. For us, such realizations are indeed among the positive outgrowths of growing older.

Reconstructing the Experience of Loss

The death of someone dear can confront us with a sense of inalterable deficit—hopelessness, fear and remorse. It can even lead to anger and revenge. However, loss is not only loss. At least, that is the message of Robert Neimeyer's recent volume, *Meaning Reconstruction and the Experience of Loss*. As this collection of 17 contributions—by therapists and scholars—makes clear, death does not in itself constitute loss or trigger debilitating grief. Rather, it challenges survivors to engage in a complex process of constructing meaning. Often finding a positive outcome of a loss may take a long time. And even so, one may never forget the one who has died or end a sense of loss. The most uplifting message in this volume is that loss may be reconstructed in myriad ways that go beyond the negative. This possibility has long been present in many religious and spiritual traditions, and the present work underscores the value of these traditions as cultural resources. We recall that as Mary's mother was dying, she treasured the idea that she would again meet her beloved spouse. Her one question to her pastor was when that would take place, immediately after dying or sometime later. He was quite reassuring that it would be sooner rather than later.

However, even in the more secular world, significant alternatives to the negative may be located. We find, for example, that death as a gift, a sacrifice, an opportunity to celebrate the life of the lost one, an opportunity to rekindle family or community ties, or a challenge to live more fully. These are all vitalizing ways of reconstructing loss. By dedicating ourselves to a more fully engaged life may also be a way of honoring of the deceased, and thus a means of daily carrying him/her within us. For us, many of our family rituals take shape in memorializing family members who have died. Certain drinks, recipes, holiday patterns and decorations are tokens of remembrance for them.

As many of these chapters also emphasize, the meaning-making process is inherently a social one. Whether we rely on social traditions or ongoing relationships, making meaning is embedded in our relationships. The importance of family and communal relations in reconstructing loss cannot be overestimated.

For more: Neimeyer Robert A. (Ed.) (2001) *Meaning Reconstruction and the Experience of Loss*. Washington, DC: American Psychological Association Press.

About the Authors

Mary Gergen, Professor Emerita, Penn State University, Brandywine, is a pioneer in the field of Performative Social Science, and an active participant in feminist psychology circles. Among her most important books are: *Feminist Reconstructions in Psychology: Narrative, Gender and Performance and Playing with Purpose: Adventures in Performative Social Science* (with K. Gergen). She has been actively engaged in research and writing on the aging process for over four decades. Mary is also a co-founder and a member of the Executive Board of the Taos Institute.

Kenneth J. Gergen is a Senior Research Professor at Swarthmore College, and President of the Taos Institute. He has been a primary figure in developing social constructionist thought and relational theory in the social sciences Among his major works are *Realities and Relationships, The Saturated Self, An Invitation to Social Construction,* and, *Relational Being: Beyond Self and Community.* Gergen's work has merited numerous awards, including fellowships from the Guggenheim and Humboldt foundations, and honorary degrees in Europe and the US.

TAOS INSTITUTE PUBLICATIONS

See all the Taos Publications at
www.taosinstitute.net/taos-books-and-publications

Taos Institute Publications Books in Print

* * * * * * *

Taos Tempo Series:
Collaborative Practices for Changing Times

The Magic of Organisational Life, (2017) by Mette Vinther Larsen

Paths to Positive Aging: Dog Days with a Bone and Other Essays, (2017) by Mary Gergen and Kenneth J. Gergen

70Candles! Women Thriving in Their 8th Decade, (2015) by Jane Giddan and Ellen Cole (also available as an e-book)

U&ME: Communicating in Moments that Matter, New & Revised! (2014) by John Stewart (also available as an e-book)

Relational Leading: Practices for Dialogically Based Collaboration, (2013) by Lone Hersted and Kenneth J. Gergen (also available as an e-book)

Retiring But Not Shy: Feminist Psychologists Create their Post-Careers, (2012) edited by Ellen Cole and Mary Gergen (also available as an e-book)

Developing Relational Leadership: Resources for Developing Reflexive Organizational Practices, (2012) by Carsten Hornstrup, Jesper Loehr-Petersen, Joergen Gjengedal Madsen, Thomas Johansen, Allan Vinther Jensen (also available as an e-book)

Practicing Relational Ethics in Organizations, (2012) by Gitte Haslebo and Maja Loua Haslebo

Healing Conversations Now: Enhance Relationships with Elders and Dying Loved Ones, (2011) by Joan Chadbourne and Tony Silbert

Riding the Current: How to Deal with the Daily Deluge of Data, (2010) by Madelyn Blair

Ordinary Life Therapy: Experiences from a Collaborative Systemic Practice, (2009) by Carina Håkansson

Mapping Dialogue: Essential Tools for Social Change, (2008) by Marianne "Mille" Bojer, Heiko Roehl, Mariane Knuth-Hollesen, and Colleen Magner

Positive Family Dynamics: Appreciative Inquiry Questions to Bring Out the Best in Families, (2008) by Dawn Cooperrider Dole, Jen Hetzel Silbert, Ada Jo Mann, and Diana Whitney

* * * * * * *

Focus Book Series

A Student's Guide to Clinical Supervision: You are not Alone, (2014) by Glenn E. Boyd (also available as an e-book)

When Stories Clash: Addressing Conflict with Narrative Mediation, (2013) by Gerald Monk, and John Winslade (also available as an e-book)

Bereavement Support Groups: Breathing Life into Stories of the Dead, (2012) by Lorraine Hedtke (also available as an e-book)

The Appreciative Organization, Revised Edition (2008) by Harlene Anderson, David Cooperrider, Kenneth J. Gergen, Mary Gergen, Sheila McNamee, Jane Watkins, and Diana Whitney

Appreciative Inquiry: A Positive Approach to Building Cooperative Capacity, (2005) by Frank Barrett and Ronald Fry (also available as an e-book)

Dynamic Relationships: Unleashing the Power of Appreciative Inquiry in Daily Living, (2005) by Jacqueline Stavros and Cheri B. Torres

Appreciative Sharing of Knowledge: Leveraging Knowledge Management for Strategic Change, (2004) by Tojo Thatchenkery

Social Construction: Entering the Dialogue, (2004) by Kenneth J. Gergen, and Mary Gergen (also available as an e-book)

Appreciative Leaders: In the Eye of the Beholder, (2001) edited by Marge Schiller, Bea Mah Holland, and Deanna Riley

Experience AI: A Practitioner's Guide to Integrating Appreciative Inquiry and Experiential Learning, (2001) by Miriam Ricketts and Jim Willis

* * * * * * *

Books for Professionals Series

Social Constructionist Perspectives on Group Work, (2015) edited by Emerson F. Rasera

New Horizons in Buddhist Psychology: Relational Buddhism for Collaborative Practitioners, (2010) edited by Maurits G.T. Kwee

Positive Approaches to Peacebuilding: A Resource for Innovators, (2010) edited by Cynthia Sampson, Mohammed Abu-Nimer, Claudia Liebler, and Diana Whitney

Social Construction on the Edge: 'Withness'-Thinking & Embodiment, (2010) by John Shotter

Joined Imagination: Writing and Language in Therapy, (2009) by Peggy Penn

Celebrating the Other: A Dialogic Account of Human Nature, (reprint 2008) by Edward Sampson

Conversational Realities Revisited: Life, Language, Body and World, (2008) by John Shotter

Horizons in Buddhist Psychology: Practice, Research and Theory, (2006) edited by Maurits Kwee, Kenneth J. Gergen, and Fusako Koshikawa

Therapeutic Realities: Collaboration, Oppression and Relational Flow, (2005) by Kenneth J. Gergen

SocioDynamic Counselling: A Practical Guide to Meaning Making, (2004) by R. Vance Peavy

Experiential Exercises in Social Construction—A Fieldbook for Creating Change, (2004) by Robert Cottor, Alan Asher, Judith Levin, and Cindy Weiser

Dialogues About a New Psychology, (2004) by Jan Smedslund

* * * * * * *

WorldShare Books—Free PDF Download

Spirituality, Social Construction and Relational Processes: Essays and Reflections (PDF version 2016) edited by Duane Bidwell.

Therapy as a Hermeneutic and Constructionist Dialogue: Practices of freedom and of deco-construction in the relational, language and meaning games (PDF version 2016) by Gilberto Limon (Translated from Spanish)

Recovered Without Treatment: The Process of Abandoning Crystal Meth Use Without Professional Help (PDF version 2016) by Pavel Nepustil

Introduction to Group Dynamics: Social Construction Approach to Organizational Development and Community Revitalization, (PDF version 2016), by Toshio Sugiman

Recursos psico-sociales para el post-conflicto" (Psico-social resources for post-conflict) (PDF version 2016), Edited by Angela Maria Estrada

Buddha As Therapist: Meditations (PDF version 2015), by G.T. Maurits Kwee

Diálogos para la transformación: experiencias en terapia y Otras intervenciones psicosociales en Iberoamérica—Volumen 1 and 2 (PDF version 2015), by Dora Fried Schnitman, Editora

Education as Social Construction: Contributions to Theory, Research and Practice (PDF version 2015) Editors: Thalia Dragonas, Kenneth J. Gergen, Sheila McNamee, Eleftheria Tseliou

Psychosocial Innovation in Post-War Sri Lanka (PDF version 2015) by Laurie Charles and Gameela Samarasinghe

Social Accountability & Selfhood (PDF version 2015, original publication date – 1984, Basil Blackwell, Inc.) by John Shotter

Construccionismo Social Y Discusion De Paradrigmas En Psicologia: Indeterminacion, Holismo y Juegos de Lenguaje vs. La Teoria Pictorica del Lenguaje (PDF versión 2015) by Roberto Aristequi

{In}Credible Leadership: A Guide for Shared Understanding and Application (PDF version 2015) by Yuzanne Mare, Isabel Meyer, Elonya Niehaus-Coetzee, Johann Roux

Etnia Terapéutica: Integrando Entornos (PDF version 2015) by Jeannette Samper A. and José Antonio Garciandía I.

Post-modern Education & Development (Chinese edition, PDF version 2014) Introduction by Shi-Jiuan Wu (後現代教育與發展　　介紹　　吳熙珺)

Exceeding Expectations: An Anthology of Appreciative Inquiry Stories in Education from Around the World (PDF version 2014) Story Curators: Dawn Dole, Matthew Moehle, and Lindsey Godwin

The Discursive Turn in Social Psychology (PDF version 2014), by Nikos Bozatzis & Thalia Dragonas (Eds.)

Happily Different: Sustainable Educational Change—A Relational Approach (PDF version 2014), by Loek Schoenmakers

Strategising through Organising: The Significance of Relational Sensemaking, (PDF version 2013), by Mette Vinther Larsen

Therapists in Continuous Education: A Collaborative Approach, (PDF version 2013), by Ottar Ness

Contextualizing Care: Relational Engagement with/in Human Service Practices, (PDF version 2013), by Janet Newbury

Nuevos Paradigmas, Cultura y Subjetividad, by Dora Fried Schnitman

Novos Paradigmas Em Mediação (PDF versión 2013, original publicación date 1999), Dora Fried Schnitman y Stephen LittleJohn (editors)

Filo y Sofía En Diálogo: La poesía social de la conversación terapéutica (PDF version 2013, original publicación date 2000), Klaus G. Deissler y Sheila McNamee (editors). Traducción al español: Mario O. Castillo Rangel

Socially Constructing God: Evangelical Discourse on Gender and the Divine (PDF version 2013), by Landon P. Schnabel

Ohana and the Creation of a Therapeutic Community (PDF version 2013), by Celia Studart Quintas

From Nonsense Syllables to Holding Hands: Sixty Years as a Psychologist (PDF version 2013), by Jan Smedslund

Management and Organization: Relational Alternatives to Individualism (PDF version 2013, reprinted with permission) Edited by Dian Marie Hosking, H. Peter Dachler, Kenneth J. Gergen

Appreciative Inquiry to Promote Local Innovations among Farmers Adapting to Climate Change (PDF version 2013) by Shayamal Saha

La terapia Multi-Being. Una prospettiva relazionale in psicoterapia, (PDF version 2013) by Diego Romaioli

Psychotherapy by Karma Transformation: Relational Buddhism and Rational Practice (PDF version 2013) by G.T. Maurits Kwee

La terapia como diálogo hermenéutico y construccionista: Márgenes de libertad y deco-construcción en los juegos relacionales, de lenguaje y de significado (PDF versión 2012) by Gilberto Limón Arce

Wittgenstein in Practice: His Philosophy of Beginnings, and Beginnings, and Beginnings (PDF version 2012) by John Shotter

Social Construction of the Person (PDF version 2012). Editors: Kenneth J. Gergen and Keith M. Davis, Original copyright date: 1985, Springer-Verlag, New York, Inc.

Images of Man (PDF version 2012, original copyright date: 1975) by John Shotter. Methuen, London.

Ethical Ways of Being (PDF version 2012). By Dirk Kotze, Johan Myburg, Johann Roux, and Associates. Original copyright date: 2002, Ethics Alive, Institute for Telling Development, Pretoria, South Africa.

Piemp (PDF version 2012), by Theresa Hulme. Published in Afrikaans.

For book information and ordering, visit Taos Institute Publications at:
www.taosinstitutepublications.net

For further information, call: 1-888-999-TAOS, 1-440-338-6733
Email: info@taosinstitute.net

CPSIA information can be obtained
at www.ICGtesting.com
Printed in the USA
BVHW010259060620
580778BV00007BA/363

9 781938 552502